PLANS OF ARCHITECTURE

BUILDING DETAILS

Author	Editorial manager	Project coordinator
Francisco Asensio Cerver	Paco Asensio	Ivan Bercedo (Architect)

Design and layout	Translation & Proofreading	
Mireia Casanovas Soley	Amber Ockrassa	

Photographers

Georges Fessy (*Lille Fine Arts Palace*); Paul Groh (*Samitaur*); David Cardelús (*Rubi Station*); Naito Architect & Assoc. (*Seafolk Museum*); Architeckturphoto (*Exhibition Center in Leipzig*); Tino Martínez (*Galician Contemporary Arts Center*); Tim Hursley (*Corning Child Development Center*); Georges Fessy (*Music Museum*); Christian Kandzia (*Bundestag*), Renzo Piano (*Cy twombly Annex*)

1998 ◉ Francisco Asensio Cerver   ISBN:0-8230-7188-X   Printed in Spain

Published by:

Whitney Library of Design
an imprint of Watson and Guptill Publications/New York
1515 Broadway
New York-NY 10036 USA

The number of publications dedicated to Architecture have increased considerably in the last few years. This shows not only society's growing interest in the city's image and therefore the look of its buildings, but also interest on the part of professionals in familiarizing themselves with their colleagues work in every corner of the planet and in staying informed on new materials and technical solutions. In spite of the quantity of already existing books on architecture, there was nevertheless a need to delve deeper than the finished projects, to analyze the creative process and the technical solutions chosen. *Plans of Architecture* was created with this idea in mind.

On the following pages, some of modern Architecture's most significant works are studied from rough sketches to detailed layouts. *Plans of Architecture* is therefore destined to be used as a work tool as well as for general interest. The examples herein detailed constitute a clear reference for anyone wanting to use similar materials in their own work.

A short text by the architects themselves prefaces each article. The plans are drawn to scale for easy measurement comparison. Constructive details come with a key in which each material is specified. Similarly, photographs have been chosen which augment the graphic documentation in order to better represent the look of the finished product.

In identifying with the Architectural vision from a professional point of view, *Plans of Architecture: Building Details* shows strength rarely seen in the publishing world.

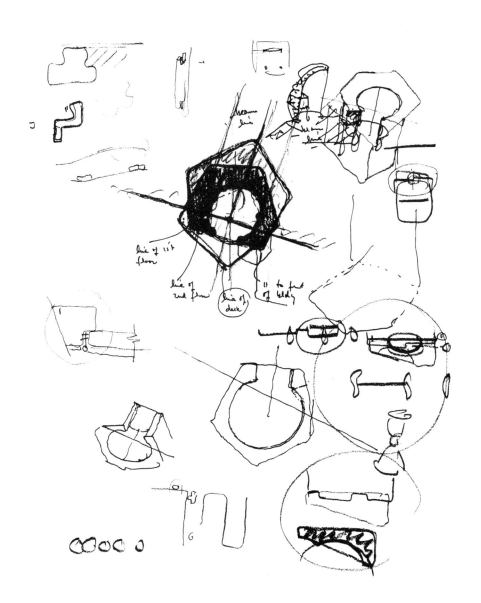

Lille Fine Arts Palace

Jean Marc Ibos & Mirto Vitart

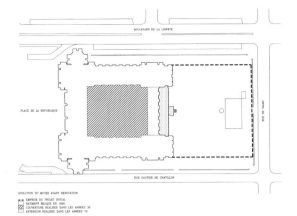

EVOLUTION DU MUSEE AVANT RENOVATION
EMPRISE DU PROJET INITIAL
BATIMENT REALISE EN 1895
COUVERTURE REALISEE DANS LES ANNEES 30
EXTENSION REALISEES DANS LES ANNEES 70

Architects: *Jean-Marc Ibos and Myrto Vitart*
Site: *Lille, France.*
Surface area: *300,000sq.ft.in total, of which 118,000sq.ft. are of new construction.*
Dates: *March 1990 (competition)*
1990-92 (plan of execution)
1992-97 (construction)

Associates: *Pierre Cantacuzène (coordinator), Sophie Nguyen (façades of the palace and museography)*
Structure: *Ingeniería Khephren*
Façades: *Y.R.M. Antony Hunt &Ass.*
Installations: *Ingeniería Alto*
Client: *Lille City Council*
Financing: *Public. FF150 million for the building and FF30 million for the museography project.*
Construction: *Lille City Council.*

The bases of the competition contemplated not only the renovation of the existing building and its adaptation to current standards, but the possibility of a complete rethinking of the way the existing collections were exhibited. In addition, there were to be a new room for temporary exhibitions, an auditorium, a library and educational workshops and the reorganisation of the museum´s conservation service with the creation of new technical workshops. In all it was envisaged that about 54,000sq.ft. of exhibition space would be added to the existing183,000sq.ft.

The Palace was constructed in 1895 and was a reduced version of a more ambitious design by Berard and Delmas in the style of the Musée del Louvre. The original plan called for a building twice the built size. This would have filled the site now occupied by the new construction of Ibos and Vitart, winners of the modern competition. Ironically, these architects have chosen to cover one side of their new building with a screen of glass which reflects the old palace, doubling its image, and thereby redeeming the idea of the original design. "We wanted to go towards the meaning of the building, with the idea of benefitting from its qualities," explain the architects.

Undoubtedly, the most important elements in the interplay of perspectives and reflections that the two architects have created are the new screen/building, and the false pond, also made of glass, which opens and closes electronically and forms the roof of the new room for temporary exhibitions. The background of this perspective is formed by the north façade of the new extension; a succession of superimposed vertical planes. The first is a plane of glass on which a design of tiny mirrors reflects an impressionistic image of the original building. Behind, there are gold -colored chromium-plated panels on a red background. The façade, like the south façade of the same building, is formed by double-glazed glass panels, either fixed or opening, separated by an air chamber. The glass panels are fixed by screws to a network of aluminium mounts and crosspieces, which are anchored to the concrete by ties of stainless steel. In the north façade, the air conditioning pipes and the fibre optic cable for lighting control run between the concrete and the glass panels.In the south façade, a system of sensors measures direct sunlight, temperature and wind speed and automatically controls a system of external awnings. The special feature of the horizontal glass which forms the false pond is the slightness of its inclination (1%) and the dimensions of its glass panels (18 x 3 feet each), supported by a network of steel profiles, in turn supported by six 62-foot steel beams, which cross the room on its short side. Between the beams, another automatic system controls sunlight and adapts the level of natural light to the requirement of the works on exhibition.

Site plan in which can be appreciated the structuring function acquired by the Palace's courtyard between Republic Square and the glazed square.

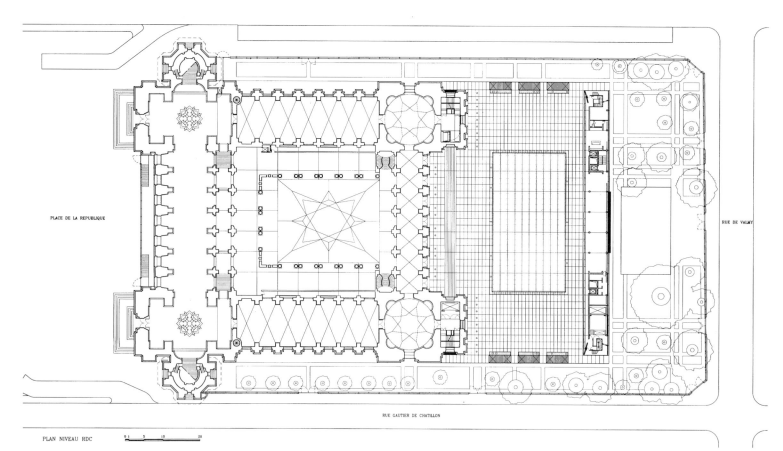

PLACE DE LA REPUBLIQUE

RUE DE VALMY

RUE GAUTIER DE CHATILLON

PLAN NIVEAU RDC   0 1   5   10   20

Ground floor. Both of the rotundas nearest to the glazed plaza are almost completely filled by the enormous chandeliers by Pesce. The Palace is entered from the Republic Square.

Plan of the first subterranean level, with temporary exhibition rooms under horizontal glasswork and the " relief plans" on exhibition under the atrium. Also shown is the connection between the Palace and the new conservation workshops.

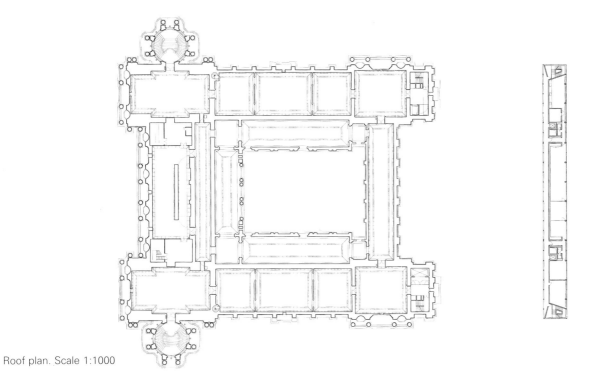

Roof plan. Scale 1:1000

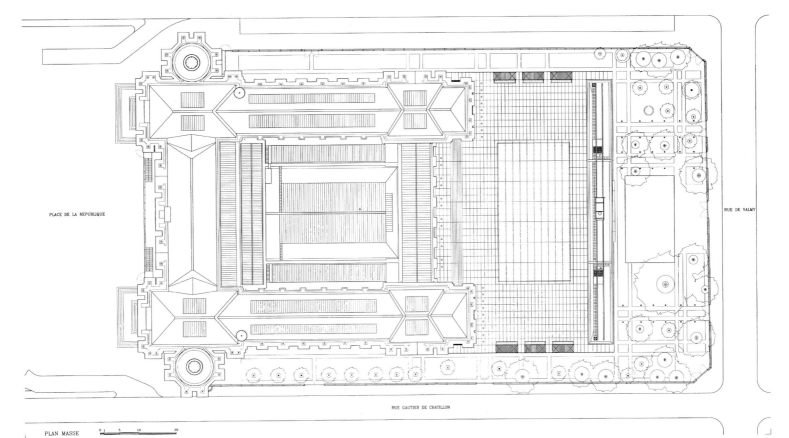

PLACE DE LA REPUBLIQUE

RUE DE VALMY

RUE GAUTIER DE CHATILLON

PLAN MASSE   0 1   5   10   20

NUE GAUTIER DE CHATILLON

BO

Cross section of the Palace through the atrium which the renovation has turned into a covered plaza.

1/500

Cross section of the temporary exhibition rooms. The six main beams of the glass roof are aligned on the axes of the arcades of the façade of the Palace.

1/500

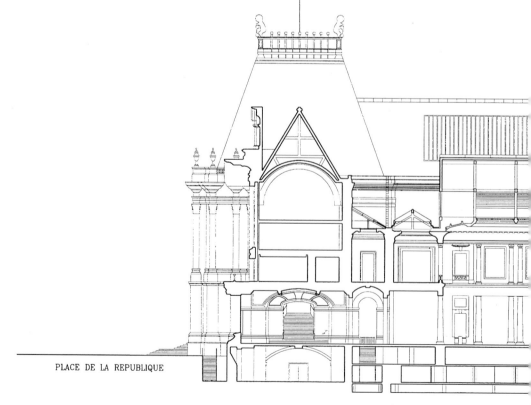

PLACE DE LA REPUBLIQUE

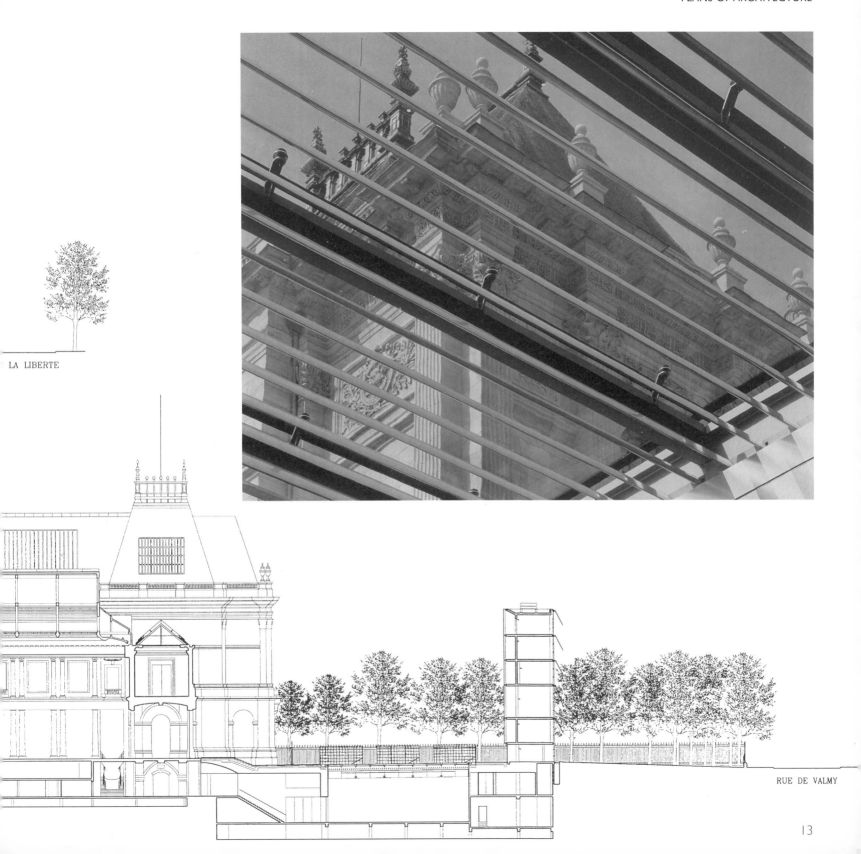

LA LIBERTE

RUE DE VALMY

Section of the north façade of the new screen/building.

1. Profile of aluminium.
2. Engraved Climalit glass, 10 mm; air chamber, 15 mm; tempered laminated glass, 66.4mm.
3. Climalit, 88,2 mm.
4. Concrete panels, 230 mm.
5. Polished concrete slab, 80 mm.
6. PVC floor lining.
7. Metal border.
8. Cornice of Alucobond aluminium sheeting, 4 mm.
9. Mineral wool.
10. Eliptic ties of stainless steel which form the structural support of the façade between each level.
11. Plate fixing the tubing.
12. Galvanized steel sheeting, 30/10.
13. Steel sheeting 20/10.
14. Grating of stainless steel.
15. Galvanized steel sheeting 20/10.
16. Plate of galvanized steel, 10mm.
17. Articulated anchor bolt fixing the glass panel.
18. Joint of black silicone, double barrier.
19. Fixing bolt of stainless steel.
20. Joints of black medium density polyethylene.
21. Grating of stainless steel.
22. Conduction tube.

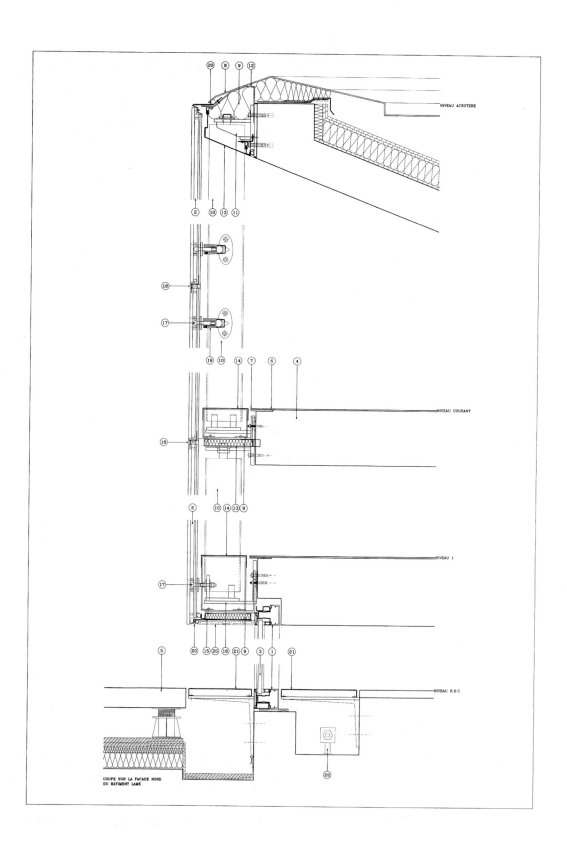

Section of the south façade of the screen/building.

1. Profile of aluminium.
2. Matrix glass, 4 mm: Planitherm sheet, 6mm; air chamber, 10 mm; Reeded glass, 6 mm.
3. Aluminium tie.
4. Concrete pillar.
5. Concrete panel, 230 mm.
6. Layer of cement.
7. Expansion joint of black medium density polyethylene.
8. Regulating screw.
9. Cornice of aluminium sheeting, Alucobond, 4 mm.
10. Mineral wool.
11. Galvanized steel sheeting 20/10.
12. Grating of stainless steel.
13. Kerbing.
14. Ventilation grate of aluminium.
15. Self-regulating grate.
16. Stainless steel plate supporting the exterior awnings, 8 mm.
17. Stainless steel plate, 8 mm.
18. Support tube of stainless steel, diameter 70 mm, 4 mm.
19. Plate of stainles steel, 8 mm.
20. Motor tube.
21. Arm of the awning.
22. Load-bearing bar of stainless steel, diameter 25 mm.
23. Strengthened fabric of white PVC.

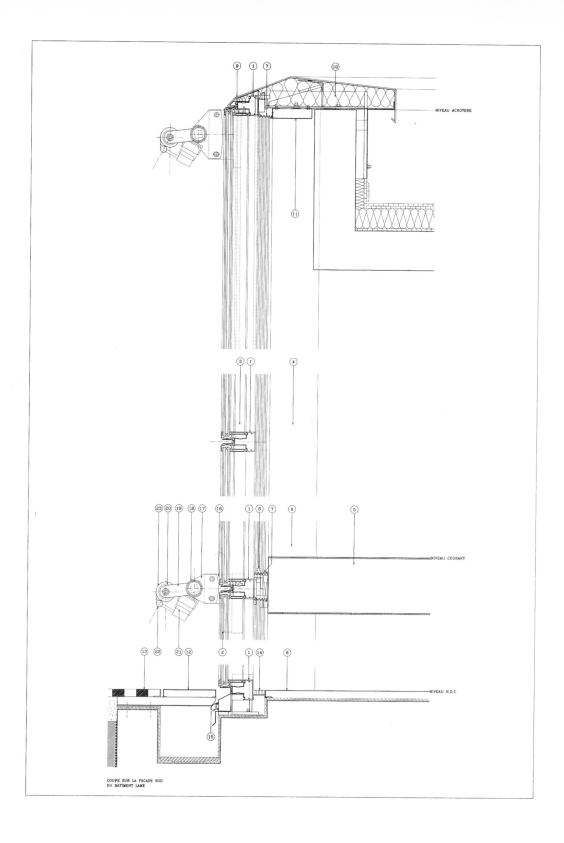

COUPE SUR LA FACADE SUD
DU BATIMENT LAME

Cross section of the horizontal glasswork.

1. Climalit, 15 mm.
2. Air chamber, 15 mm.
3. Tempered laminated glass10/10/4mm.
4. Joint of black silicone.
5. Frame of medium density polyethylene.
6. Swivel .
7. Laminated steel clamp joined to the UPN 150 profile by bolts.
8. UPN 150 soldered onto laminated steel sheets.
9. UPN 150 soldered onto steel underpinning.
10. Bridging element.
11,12 Silver blinds in open and closed positions.
13. Grey lacquered steel profile supporting the blinds.
14. Electric jack, elevated.
15. Conduit box.
16. Main beam of steel.
17. 3 mm steel sheathing of the main beams.
18. Steel tubing 30 x 30 x 2mm.
19. Steel tubing for support 50 x 30 x 2 mm.
20. Air conditioning conduit.
21. Lineal diffuser.
22. Fibreglass, 25 mm.
23. Protective sheathing.
24. Ventilation conduit.
25. Steel sheeting, 3 mm.
26. Protective sheathing 4 mm.
27. 30% perforated sheeting,3 mm.
28. Ipso adjustable lamp.
29. Erco low tension embedded halogen light.
30. Very low tension projector with shutter framing, mounted on rails.

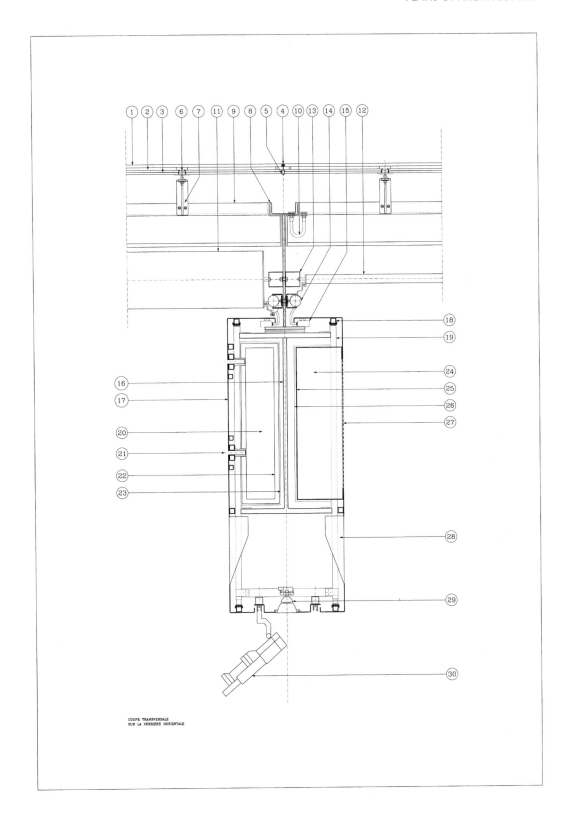

COUPE TRANSVERSALE
SUR LA VERRIERE HORIZNTALE

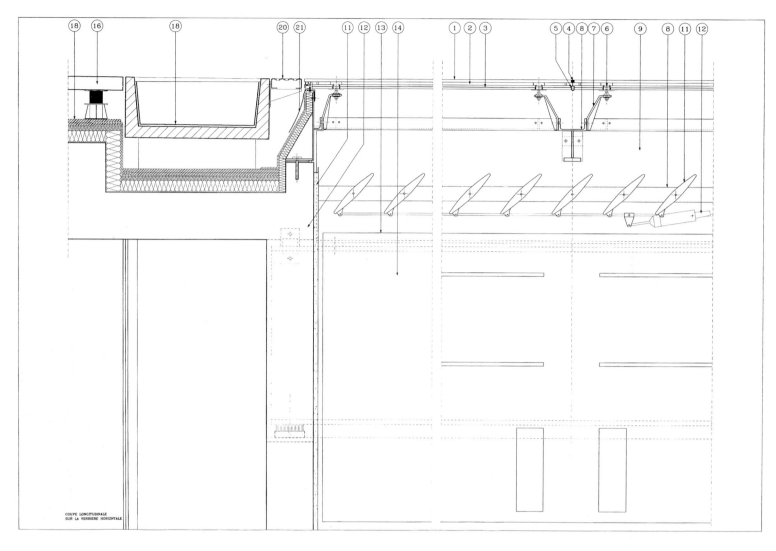

COUPE LONGITUDINALE
SUR LA VERRIERE HORIZNTALE

Longitudinal section of the horizontal glasswork.

1. Climalit,15 mm
2. Air Chamber, 15 mm
3. Tempered laminated glass, 10/10/4mm.
4. Joint of black silicone
5. Frame of medium density polyethylene which complements the waterproofing of the silicone joints, carrying any infiltrating moisture to the UPN 150 profiles which act as gutters.
6. Swivel

7. Clamps of laminated steel which are joined to the UPN 150 profile by bolts.
8. UPN 150 soldered over sheets of laminated steel.
9. Steel underpinning.
10. Profile of grey lacquered steel supporting
11. Open silver blinds.
12. Electric jack, elevated.
13. Concrete structure.
14. Plaster facing.

15. 3 mm steel sheathing of the main beams.
16. Main beam of steel.
17. Polished concrete slab.
18. Combination of insulation and waterproofing.
19. Polished concrete basin.
20. Grating of stainless steel.
21. Medium density polyethylene waterproofing.

Samitaur

Eric Owen Moss

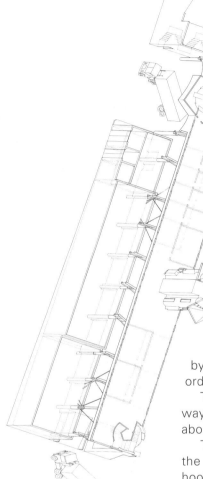

General axonometric projection.

Architect: *Eric Owen Moss*
Site: *Los Angeles. USA*
Project Architects: *Jay Vanos, Dennis Ige*
Structural Engineer: *Joe Kurily. Kurily Szymanski Tchirkow*
Mechanical Engineer: *Paul Antieri. I & N Consulting Engineer*
Construction Management: *Hannah and Associates*

"The owner asked me to do an interior addition to the sawtooth building of what came to be Samitaur. What's so wonderful about this process is that there was no site, no project, no program - it was simply a discussion of how we could provide more space for a tenant. I proposed the block in the air over the walkway.

It was an opportunity to use space in the air. The block is carried on big girders supported by pipes. That amalgamation of beams, girders, and columns, is not so much strange as is an order you couldn't anticipate.

The frame holding the block looks like (I hesitate, because this is easily misunderstood) a freeway designed by a drunk. The drunk is talking very seriously and explaining what the project is about. But he is talking in a dream. It is a drunk who sees the world precisely but differently.

The second phase of Samitaur that came along a year or two after the first phase is very much the introvert. The first phase is see and be seen - extroverted. The second phase is more covert: a hook makes a courtyard annex, and attaches to the pentagon pool.

And while the first phase was under construction, the Mayor's guys called one night and said, "Can you put another floor on Samitaur?" because they liked it. And I said, "Well, you can't put up another floor on the building because you'll screw it up and it'll fall down, but we have the Hook coming up". The Hook was originally designed to conform to the height limit which is 48 feet. And they said, "Okay, can you take the second phase, and redesign it so it clearly breaks the height limit." So the introvert now has a tower 125 feet high.

The hook and the tower should be done together. It's a steel frame, nine floors - which would certainly jump out of the site. The area isn't sacrosanct, but it has residual meaning: the new changes the old, but doesn't blot it out.

The flying block is not quite a block - I have to say. On the underside there are pieces cut away so more light gets in. The light moves and the structure dances.

The entry piece with the stair inside is variously conical, cylindrical, and a pumpkin. It got to be more pumpkin as people walked inside on the stairs.

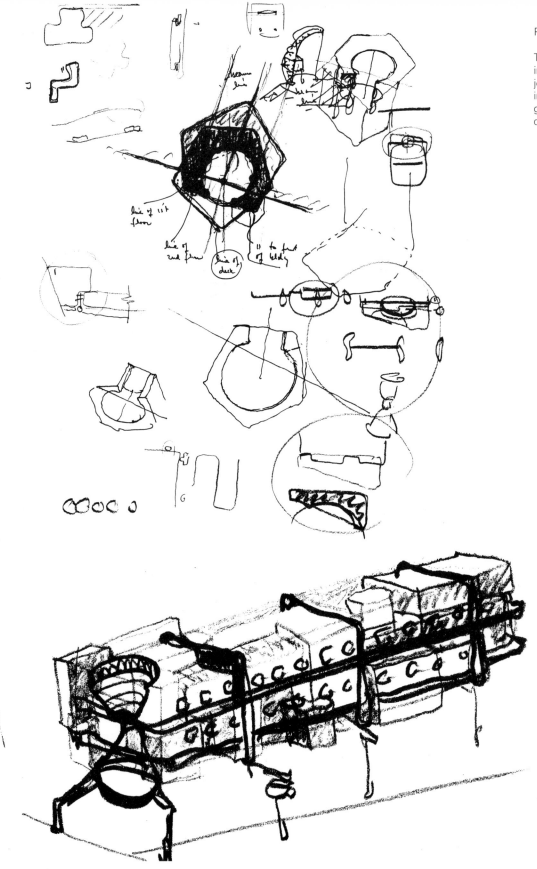

Planning sketches.

The first phase is one of the most important in Eric Owen Moss's projects. The sketches and drawings done in the first few days to a large extent generate the ideas on which his buildings are based.

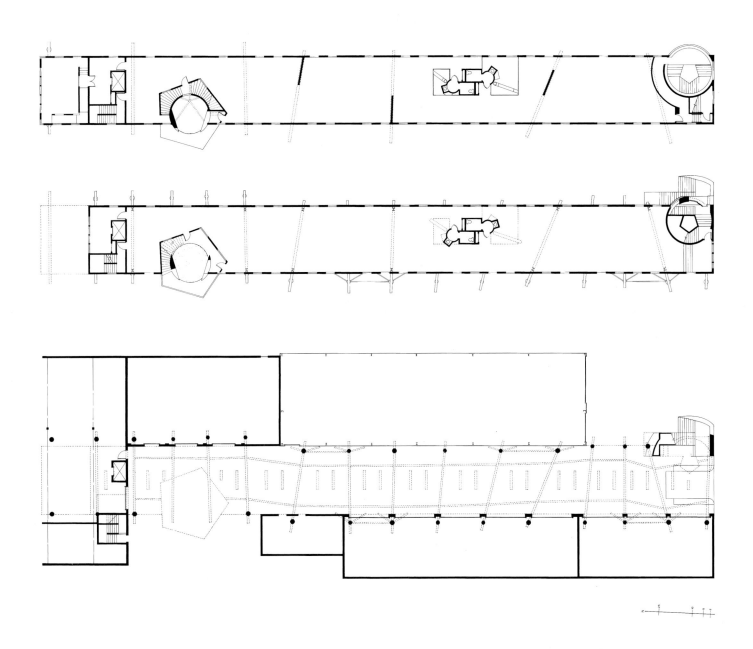

Layouts. Scale 1:500

The block is limited in height: 48 feet; in width, by the fire department: you can't cross an imaginary line over the existing block below. So the building in the air over the road is only over the road - it can't be over the adjacent buildings; underneath the block there is a required clearance of 15 feet for trucks. That's the block. So Samitaur is the block, the limits of the block, or cutting out of the block. Never adding.

The other prominent dent in the block is the pool area which is an admixture of two-five sided figures. It's not a pool that fills up like a swimming pool. It's inverted. So the water is very thin, flows to a hole, disappears, and is pumped around again.

The underside of that pool area is a bridge, part of an arched structure where columns in the original order of frame were removed so the trucks that entered at the cone could exit under the pool. The egress point is the arch, and above on the deck is a bridge over the pool. A bridge over a bridge.

The other exception to the blocks is the board room, which hops up over the old sawtooth roofs. Go in the lobby, get on the elevator, come up, and if you go toward the cone, you're in the office space on two floors. Go the opposite way and there's a floor and a half high board room which opens up to a remarkable view of Los Angeles.

Construction axonometric. The building is higher than the roofs of the warehouses in the area.

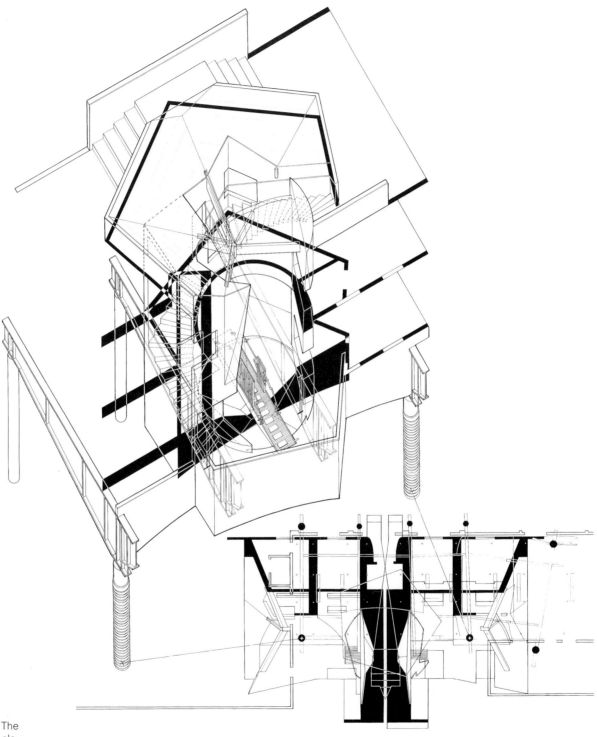

Detail of pentagonal staircase. The staircase is one of the central elements in the work of Eric Owen Moss. He almost always shakes up the design, provoking spatial complexity.

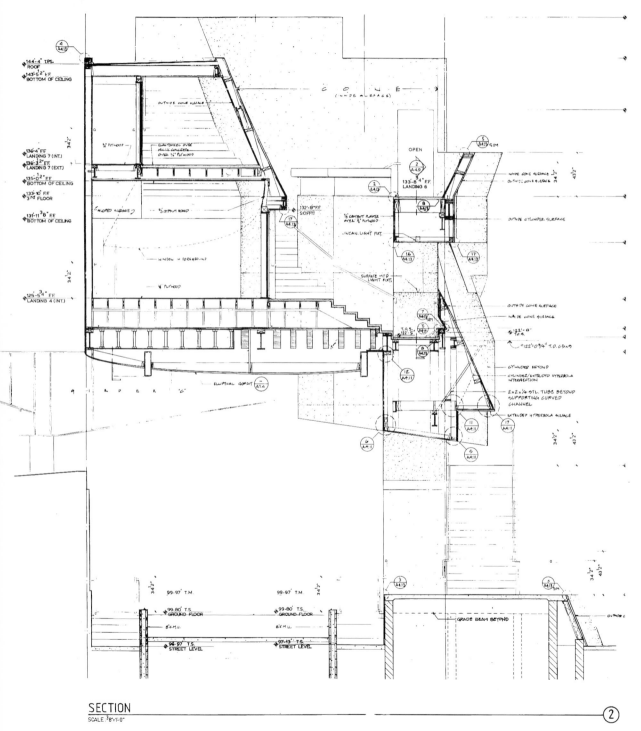

Two constructive sections of the staircase. Contrary to first impressions, the walls are not concrete; rather, their final finish is done in gray stucco.

SECTION
SCALE: 3/8"=1'-0"

(2)

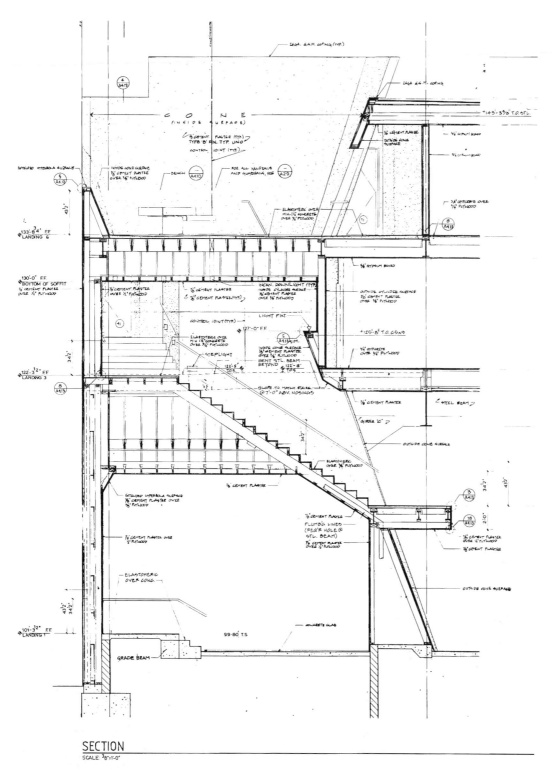

SECTION
SCALE: 3/8"=1'-0"

The ground floor is left un-built allowing space for loading, unloading and movement of trucks.

Rubi Station

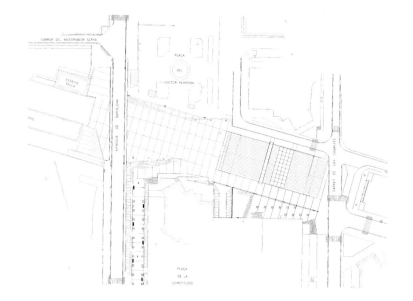

Site plan.

Architects: *Arderiu & Morato Arquitectes*
Site: *Plaza Dr.Pearson. Rubi (Espana)*
Client: *Ferrocarriles de la Generalitat de Catalunya*
Engineering: *G.P.O.*
Collaborators: *Sigfrid Pascual, Jose Martins dos Santos, Gracia Borrell, Montse Alegre.*

Rubi is a small town linked to Barcelona by new metropolitan transport systems and its railway station is by nature a way station as the trajectory does not end here. Its layout is conditioned by heavy passenger transit, the removal of a crossing at Barcelona Avenue and by the rail network which has limited the historic urban link and which is now distinguished by high isolated buildings. These characteristics separate this project from traditional train stations . It has a notable emblematic character, powerful and individualistic in opposition to the city.

Using the concept of functionality as a starting point, the architects considered the present use of intermediate stations: neutral spaces which tend to join part of the urban pattern.

In this example, the difference in height between the old crossing and Can Carbanyes Bridge led the authors to a daring decision: to place the building on the highest point and place a roof over the entire area, creating a new urban space and facilitating flow. The building is comprised of three levels which thereby allows visual communication between the spaces generated and clearly defines the scale of the wall facades. The main vestibule is a dominant feature in the entrance hall of the middle level where there are vertical accesses, like glass boxes, and the ticket window. The services area (cafeteria, shops and toilets) is arranged like bars attached to the length of the building. In this way the central zone, the waiting room, is unobstructed and has a view of the tracks which are located on the lowest level. The building's geometry corresponds to the rail network, obviating the urban fabric and creating an analogy of track activity seen from the interior. The most expressive element of the project is the roof place over the lengthened walls.

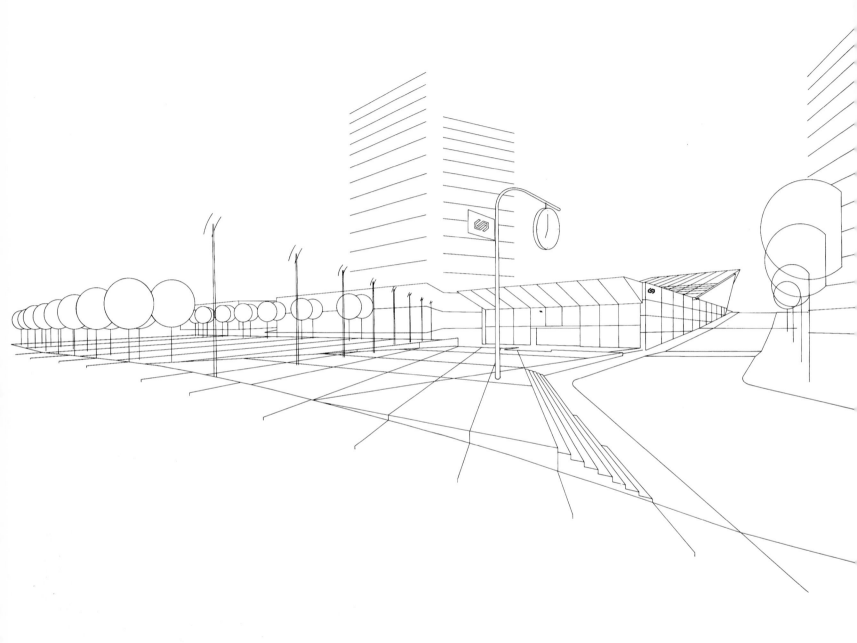

General axonometry. The Rubí (near Barcelona) train station lies next to two tall apartment buildings. Arderiu & Morató decided to take advantage of the project to order the surroundings; hence, the creation of a small square directly in front of the station.

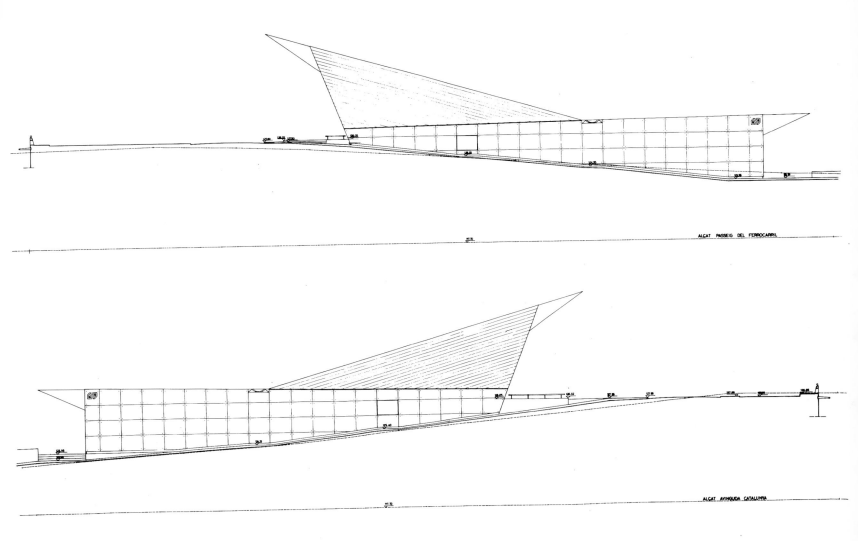

ALÇAT PASSEIG DEL FERROCARRIL

ALÇAT AVINGUDA CATALUNYA

Elevations. The architects considered the station as a continuation of the inclines of the access street and square. The roof and side walls, the defining elements of the station's image, are built with completely different materials.

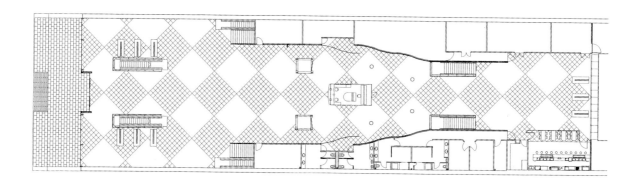

Third floor layout.

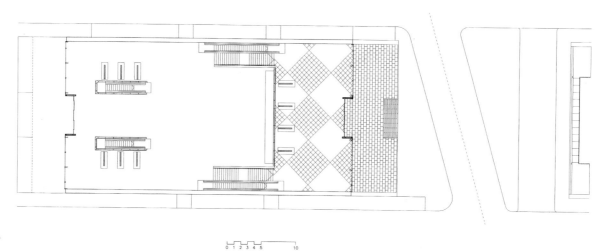

Second floor layout.

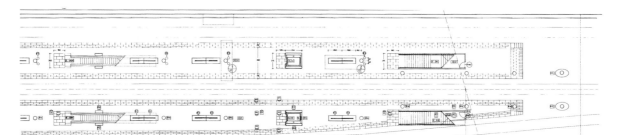

Sidewalk level layout.

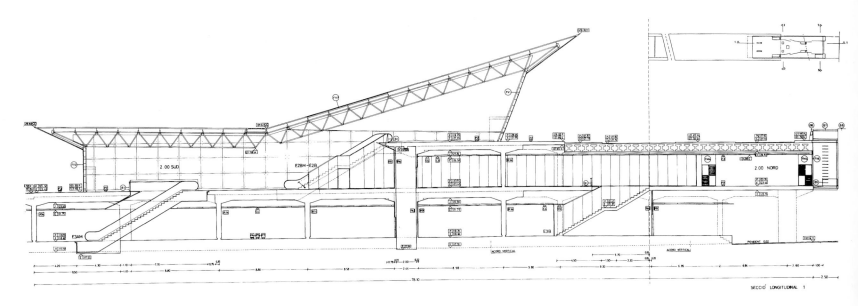

Longitudinal cross section.

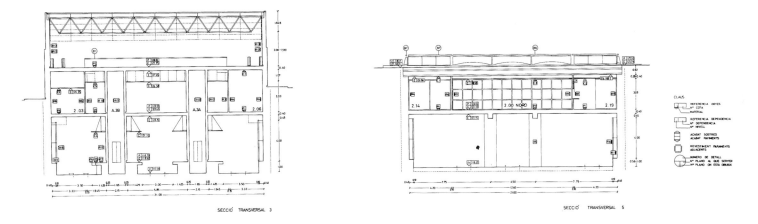

Transversal cross sections.

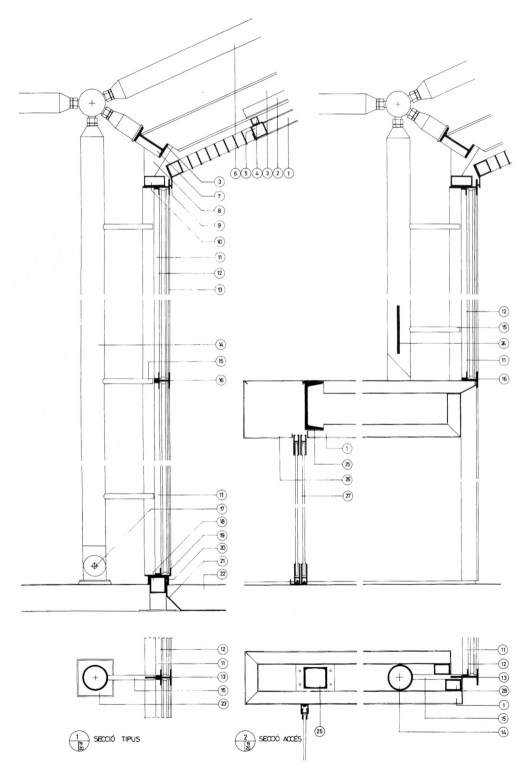

1. 50 mm. wide roof panel (Formawall 1000-v of Robertson). Hidden galvanized fastenings with gray lacquer are placed with expanded polyurethane. Silicon gasket.
2. 1 mm. galvanized steel fretted plate with white lacquer.
3. Purlins with laminated profiles (IPN 120).
4. Galvanized steel floor-boarding joists. 40 x 40 x 2 mm. tube.
5. Trox grill.
6. Orona steel mesh. Ortz joint. 2115 mm. module. 75° angle. White epoxy plastic protection.
7. 10 mm. stiffener.
8. Anchoring iron plate.
9. Stainless steel drain pipe. 1.5 mm. plate
10. 80 x 40 x 3 mm. galvanized steel rectangular tube.
11. Stainless steel strip. 25 x 25 x 3 mm. profile.
12. Glass partition of 210 x 210 cm. modules. Lower modules. Insulating glass and lamination of 3+3/12/6+6.
13. 100 x 50 x 5 mm. stainless steel profile.
14. Stainless steel connector.
16. 60 x 60 x 5 mm. stainless steel crossbeam.
17. Stainless steel ball-and-socket joint.
18. 60 x 60 x 3 mm. galvanized steel tube.
19. 100 x 30 x 5 mm. stainless steel lower crossbeam.
20. 30 X 3 mm. iron plate.
21. Double waterproofed sheet.
22. Fine grain in situ terrazzo. 100 x 100 x 3 mm. welded load bearing structure.
23. Stainless steel ball-and-socket joint.
24. support structure.
25. Sliding door support portico. UPN 180 lintel and UPN 80 pillar.
26. Sliding door fixture covers.
27. Automatic sliding door.
28. 40 x 40 x 2 mm. galvanized steel profile.
29. Galvanized steel anchorings.
30. Galvanized steel floor-boarding joists. 40 x 40 x 2 mm. tube.
31. 10 mm stamped sheet double-T profile.

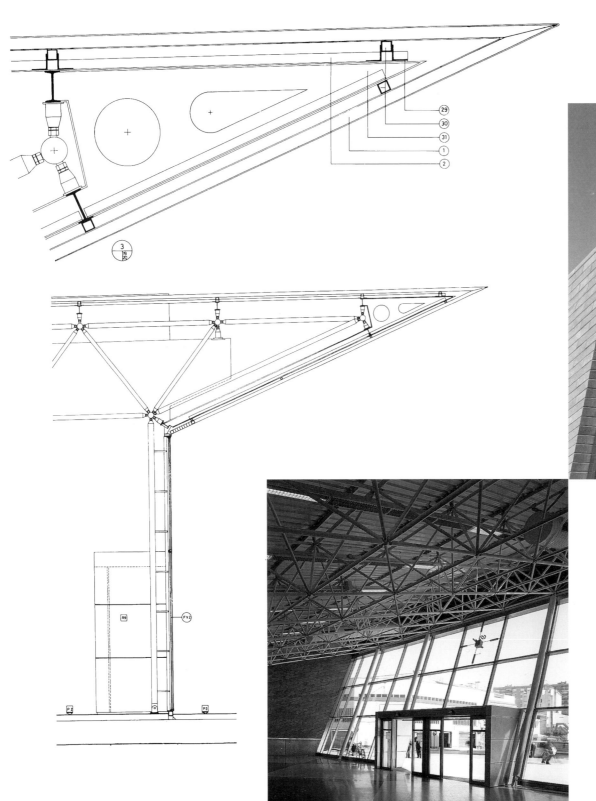

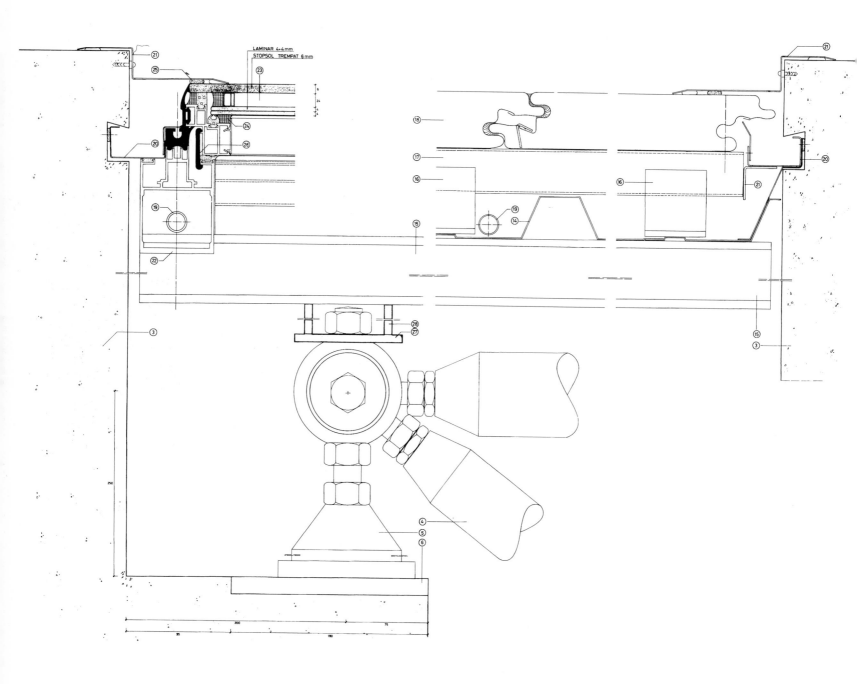

LAMINAR 4+4mm
STOPSOL TREMPAT 6mm

36

Roof and skylight detail.

1. Cast iron waterspout.
2. 25 mm. bit perforation.
3. Concrete wall.
4. Orona steel mesh. Ortz joint. 2115 mm. module. 75° angle. White epoxy plastic protection.
5. controllable mesh support.
6. 180 x 180 x 15 mm. anchoring galvanized steel plate.
7. Drainage tube embedded within the wall.
8. Galvanized steel opening with sealed gaskets.
9. Sealed gaskets.
10. Double waterproofed sheet.
11. 2 mm. lead sheet with soldered gaskets.
14. Fretted sheet of white pre-lacquered 1 mm. galvanized steel.
15. Purlins with IPN 120 profiles, protected by epoxy plastic.
16. 60 x 60 x 60 mm. galvanized steel anchorings.
17. Galvanized steel floor boarding joists. 40 x 40 x 2 mm. tube.
18. 50 mm. wide roof panel (Formawall 1000-v of "Robertson). Galvanized hidden fastenings. Silicon gasket.
19. PVC tube.
20. 1 mm. galvanized steel gutter.
21. 1 mm. pre-lacquered galvanized steel profile.
22. Base of lacquered aluminum profile.
23. Inclined skylight with 210 x 210 cm. modules. Lacquered aluminum profile. 6 mm. gray exterior plate glass. 24 mm. air chamber. 4 x 4 mm. interior polished plate glass.
24. DC-983 structural silicon.
25. M3-M6 silicon.
26. Neoprene elastic bands.
27. 100 x 100 x 10 mm. galvanized steel sheet attached to the structural node and protected by epoxy plastic.
28. IPN 100.

Seafolk Museum

Hiroshi Naito

Architect: *Hiroshi Naito.*
Site: *Japan*
Collaborators: *Hitoshi Watanabe, Nobuharu Kawamura,*
Kunio Watanabe.

Hiroshi Naito's work is sober and characterized by a clear absence of rhetoric. The basis of his projects is rationality free of dogmatism. Shapes show simple geometry and structural clarity, while materials are left unmanipulated.

Rather than decisions being made depending on individual conditions, it is obvious from the first sketches of this museum that all of the decisions have been made with a definite direction in mind, that of an underlying proto-form. Considering the objects contained in the museum (wooden fishing boats ranging from a rudimentary hollow-trunk canoe to more complicated larger models), this proto-form was easily identified as that of a boat. The museum's interior resembles the belly of a whale, while some visitor's see it as the keel of a boat. The exterior is like a "Kura", a traditional Japanese warehouse; the interior exhibition hall calls to mind a large "Naya", a typical Japanese-style barn. These are images which form the project's origins and which are now perceived by museum visitors.

The warehouse (structurally similar to a "Kura") is of prefabricated concrete with traditional tiles on the roof. The site's proximity to the sea, and therefore rapid deterioration caused by salt water, prevented the use of metal materials.

The keel-shaped volume is the product of considering the forces to which it is exposed. The resulting shape of the exhibition hall shows these forces converging at one high point from which originate a number of floor-to-ceiling ribs. Although naturally obtaining an organic image, decisions and resulting form were all strictly made according to issues of rationality and economy.

"When I take people to this museum, each one seems to imagine various things. The inside of a whale's stomach, or the keel of a ship. The exterior of the repository resembles that of a Kura, *a traditional Japanese warehouse, and the exhibition hall is a large* Naya, *a Japanese style barn."*
Hiroshi Naito.

North elevation.

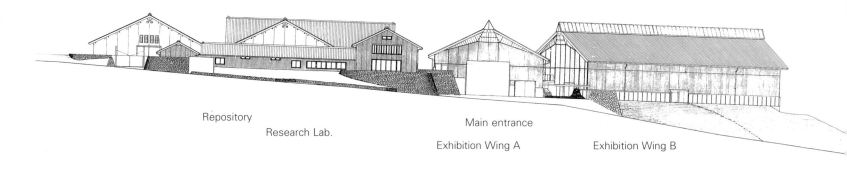

Repository

Research Lab.

Main entrance

Exhibition Wing A

Exhibition Wing B

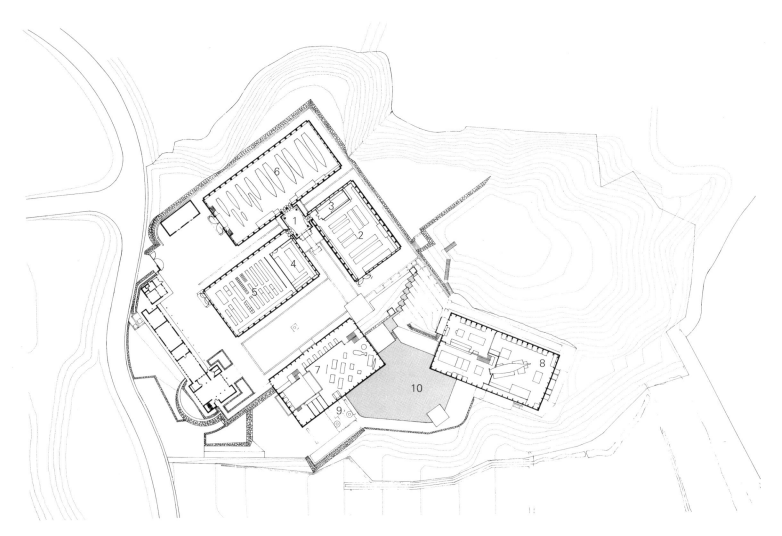

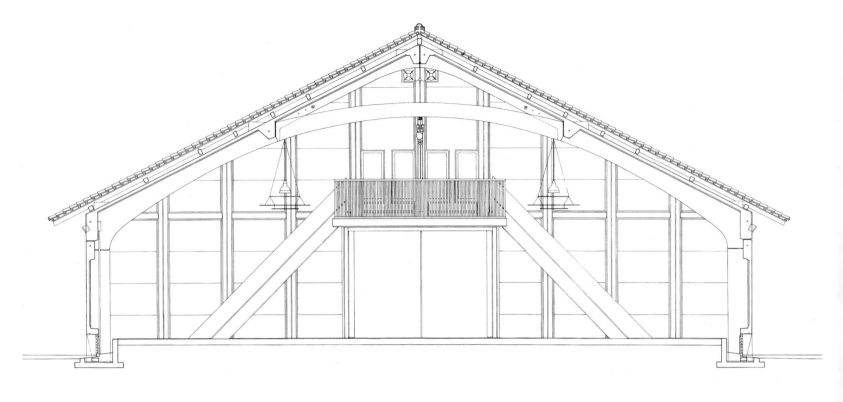

Wing A

Site plan

Repository

1. Entrance room
2. Room A (fishing nets storage)
3. Room B (storage of clothes, papers)
4. Room C (storage of tubs, casks, baskets)
5. Room D (fishing tools storage)
6. Room E (ships storage)

Exhibition hall
7. Wing A
8. Wing B
9. Main entrance
10. Water plaza
11. Courtyard

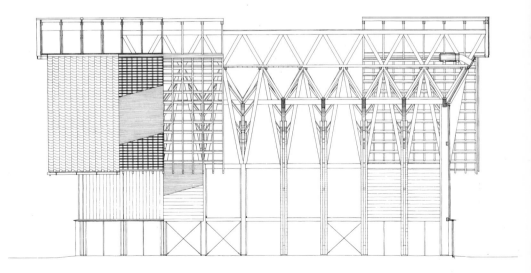

Construction scheme of the exhibition hall.

While the look of the interior and the wood structure may evoke traditional buildings, the architect himself affirms that the design of the wooden ribs and construction techniques were chosen strictly because of economic and functional criteria.

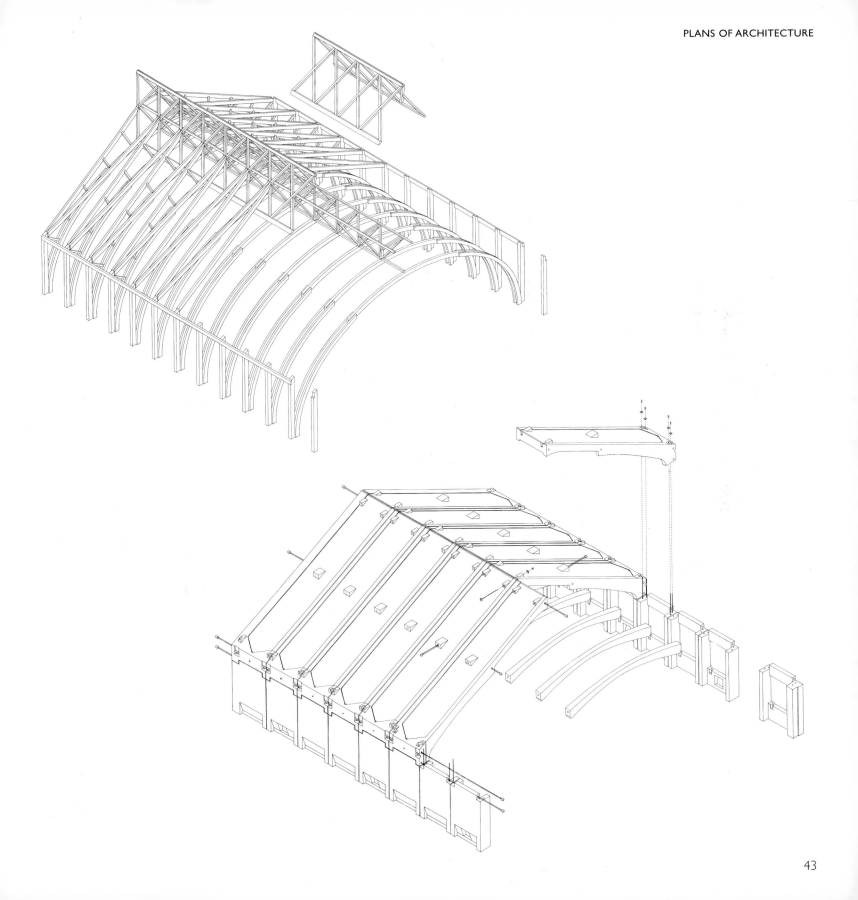

Section of Wing B.

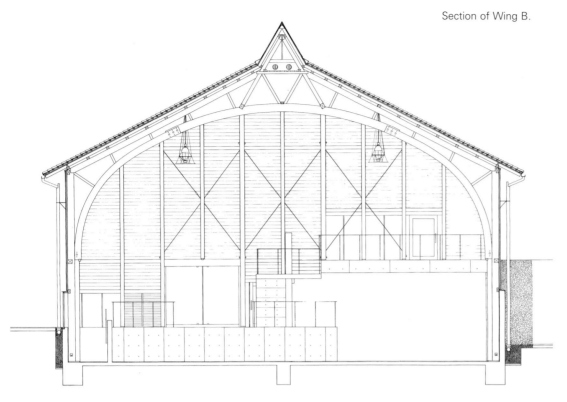

Façade detail

1. Roof construction:
   Tiles with laths.
   Seal sheeting.
   Counter battens 35 x 45 mm.
   Thermal insulation 45 mm.
   Cladding 15 mm pine.
   Rafters 60 x 120 mm.
   Rafter purlin 120 x 150 mm.

2. Wall construction:
   32 mm vertical pine cladding.
   Seal sheeting.
   Horizontal pine cladding.

3. Decking:
   Reinforced concrete base.
   3mm aluminium panel.

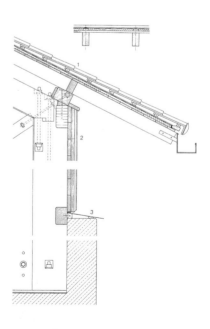

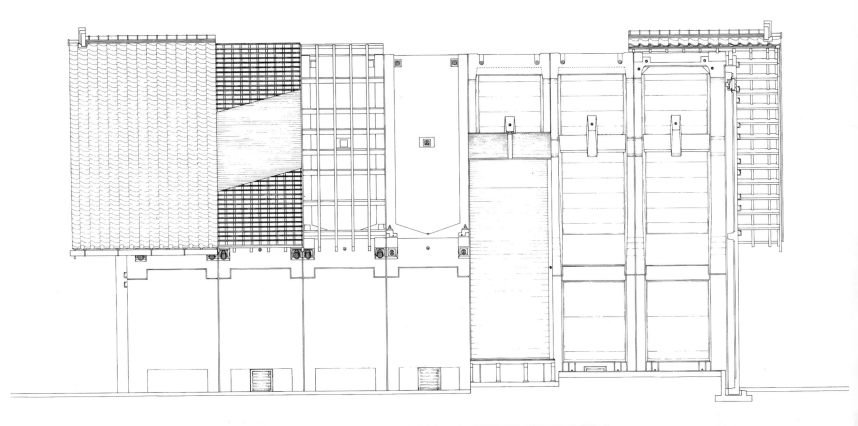

Repository construction scheme.

The museum's construction progressed in various phases. The warehouses were built first, being completed in 1989. The exhibition pavilions were finished three years later.

Exhibition Center in Leipzig

Von Gerkan + Marg

Architect: *Von Gerkan + Marg.*
Location: *Leipzig. Germany.*
Building Area: *215.000 gross square feet.*
Client: *Leipzig Messegesellschaft mbH.*
Structural Engineer: *HL-Technik, Ian Ritchie Architects.*
Landscape Architecture: *Wehberg, Eppinger, Schmidtke.*

The construction of this new exhibition center in Leipzig was considered to be the political pilot project for restructuring in the East of Germany: first prize and planning commission (implementation) through international competition, where 18 participants were invited amongst whom were, Behnisch + Partner, Richard Rogers Partnership, OMA, Storch+Ehlers and Jourdan+Muller.

The site is located at the intersection of the routes to the airport, railway, motorway and the secondary roadsystem. Here, on the former airfield site, a new urban-commercial district has been created. The linear exhibition park is built on an excavated site, of some two kilometers length, 150 meters width and 5 meters depth, which connects the existing railway station to the west, and the visitor's parking to the east, piercing through the exhibition area. This allows the architecture of the buildings and the exhibition park to form a whole.

The architects have taken up an architectural motif from the heyday of Leipzig as an exhibition city. The big, reflecting sea refers to the "Volkerschlachtsdenkmal" and the large vaulted glass roof construction picks up the motif of the Leipzig railway station, which is still the largest in Europe. The vaulted glass is a direct reference to the "Crystal Palaces" of the 19th Century and becomes the heart of the park. The archetypal form of the barrel vault, of some 250 meters length by 30 meters height and 80 meters in width, represents the "State of the Art" of glass-steel construction at the end of the 20th Century.

Frameless glass panels which are held in place at nodal points dematerialize this monumental internal space. The external spaceframe vault is a complete self-loading shell construction, which is further stabilised against wind and snow loadings with additional tie vaults (members), every 25 meters.

The square exhibition halls have a total area of 215,000 square feet. They are totally air conditioned and are devised as darker exhibition studios. They can be accessed by lorries through the large vertically sliding gateways, and can be further divided by sliding partition walls.

A convention center provides conference halls for congresses and presentations. The significant chimney tower is an 80 meter high landmark, comparable to a "campanile". Its elegant steel frame is analogous to the glasshall, which visualises the ingenious structure of sheer and bending junctures. Its traditional emblem "MM" stood for "Muster-Messe", which means exemplary exhibition, in the future it is going to represent the Leitmotif of the design concept as a human exhibition.

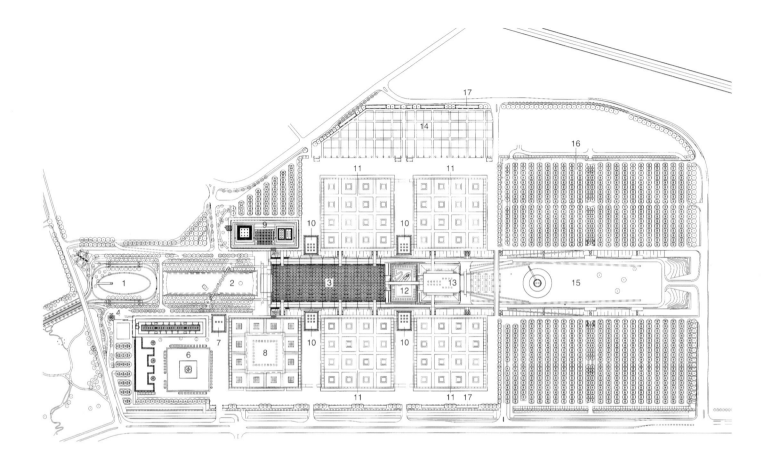

Site plan. Scale 1:8000

1. Fairground entrance.
2. Pond.
3. West entrance pavilion.
4. Tower.
5. Administration.
6. Craft center.
7. Forum.
8. Pavilion.
9. Conference hall.
10. Restaurant.
11. Exhibition pavilion.
12. Park.
13. East entrance pavilion.
14. Open air exhibitions.
15. East park.
16. Parking lot.
17. Installations.

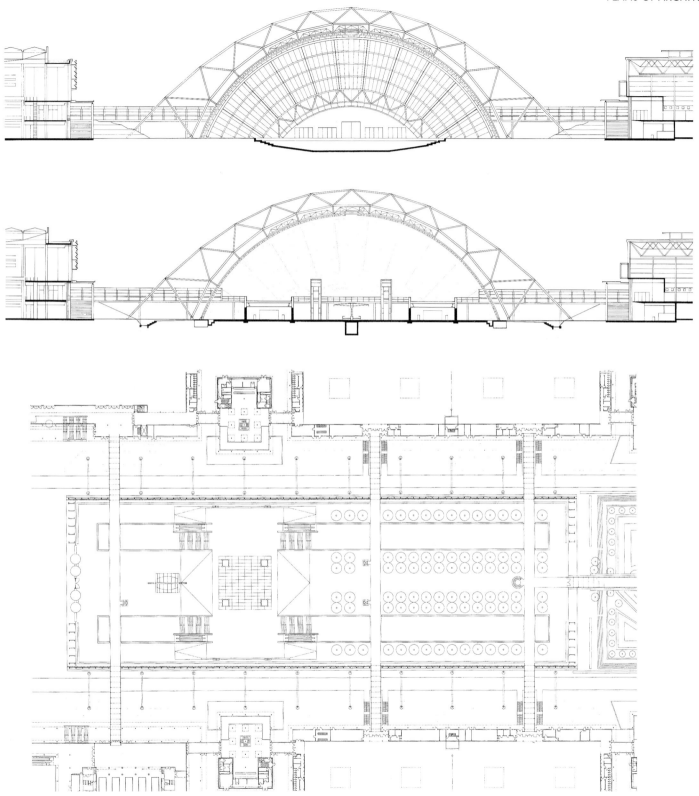

Detail.

Construction section of the central
pavilion. Scale 1:100
Delivery area with ventilation strips.

1. Steel tube, 473 X 16mm.
2. Steel tube, 244.5 X 8mm.
3. Steel tube, 318 X 12.5mm.
4. 3 mm bolt.
5. Sliding support.
6. 10 mm ESG glass strips.
7. Rotation axis.

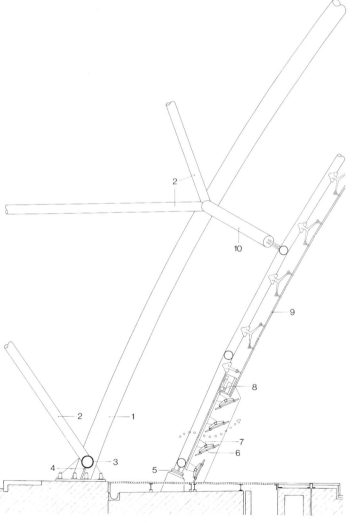

1. Steel tube, 88.9 x 7.1mm.
2. Cast metal support.
3. Fastening.
4. 6 and 8 mm. VSG glass.
5. Strut cable, 16 mm.
6. Anchor.
7. Bolt.
8. Bolt.
9. 2 mm. sheet cladding.
10. Corbel for maintenance trolley.
11. Metal strip handrail.
12. Metal section.
13. 'Sandwich' panel.
14. 3 mm. gutter with 50 mm.
    insulation and asphalt.
15. Sheet metal facade.

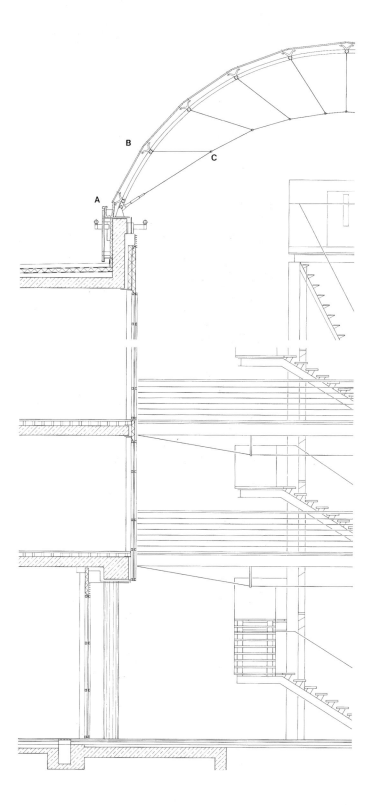

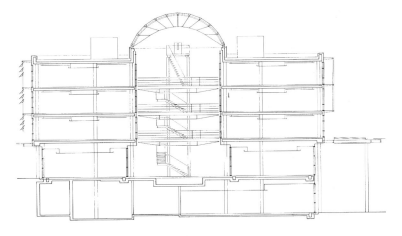

Partial section of south facade.
Scale 1:25

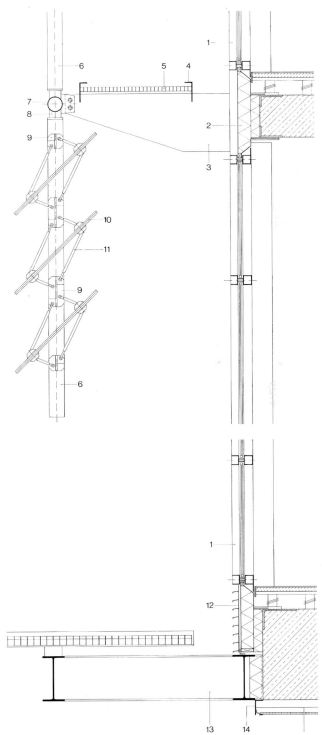

1. Aluminum reticular closing.
2. Metal panel of facade.
3. 10mm. metal corbel.
4. 50 x 130 x 5mm. steel angle.
5. Steel bar.
6. Steel tube, 108 x 2.9mm.
7. Horizontal steel tube, 108 x 4.5
8. Link.
9. Fastening.
10. 2X8mm ESG glass strips.
11. Galvanized steel brace.
12. Metal handrail.
13. IPE 300 steel beam.
14. Galvanized steel angle, 100 X 50mm.

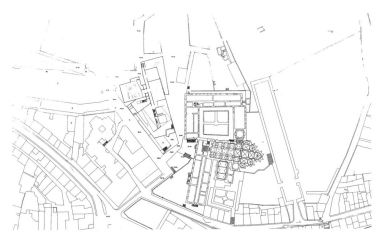

Architect: *Alvaro Siza*
Location: *Santiago de Compostela. Spain*
Area: *7,719 m²*
Estimated project cost: *2,200,000.000 spanish pesetas.*

The architect's proposal expresses the intention of restructuring a now destroyed pre-existent order by using the transformative method which precisely falls within the realm of responsibility of a contemporary art center (Centro Gallego de Arte Contemporaneo). Such reasoning necessitates a careful study of volumes, materials and languages.

The difficulty in the development of the project focuses on its insertion into a space slowly being taken over by buildings of different scales and purposes, only partially and descriptively related.

It falls to the CGAC to mediate these problematic relationships, transforming a grouping of spaces and buildings into a coherent pattern.

Preservation-transformation criteria particularly concerns the selection of cladding materials. Sheet granite with variations in color was opted for on the exterior. The use of granite takes on the expression of the very constructive system which it is subordinate to, which here refers to a reinforced concrete structure characterized by the use of large open gaps. The building is comprised of two L-shaped bodies of three floors (with accessible terrace) which lie following a north-south direction, converging in the south. Public entrances are on the first and second floors.

The west wing includes the access portico, reception and distribution zones and the entrance to the auditorium and to the second floor where there is an access vestibule to the library and documentation and administration centers.

The east wing houses exhibition space in the basement, and on the first floor are a book shop, cafeteria, the auditorium (3,945 square foot), temporary exhibit space (7,620 square foot) and various functional rooms.

The triangular space between the two bodies is a transition zone lit from above in which the entrance door and exhibit halls are situated.

The third floor internal service areas comprise an area of 20,515 square foot. The management office and administrative functions are on the first floor.

The terrace (10,290 square foot), over the east wing, is open to the public and may be used for sculptural exhibitions. The walls are 3.20 meters, as is the third floor on the south end, thereby allowing for the creation of a lookout over the city.

Site plan.

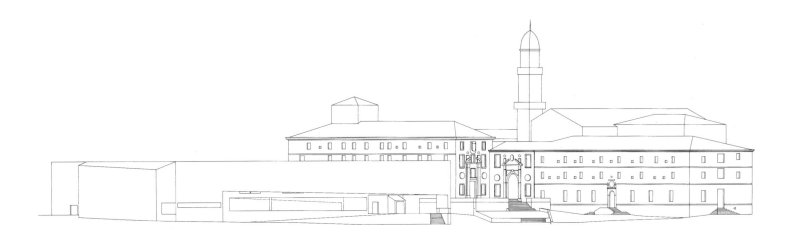

West elevation.

The Galician Center of Contemporary Art lies in the historic center of Santiago de Compostela, a city with an important architectural heritage. The building, designed by Alvaro Siza, is next to the Santo Domingo de Bonaval Convent on a recently opened street. With such defined surroundings the siting of the project becomes one of the most important decisions.

On the following page,
various cross sections.

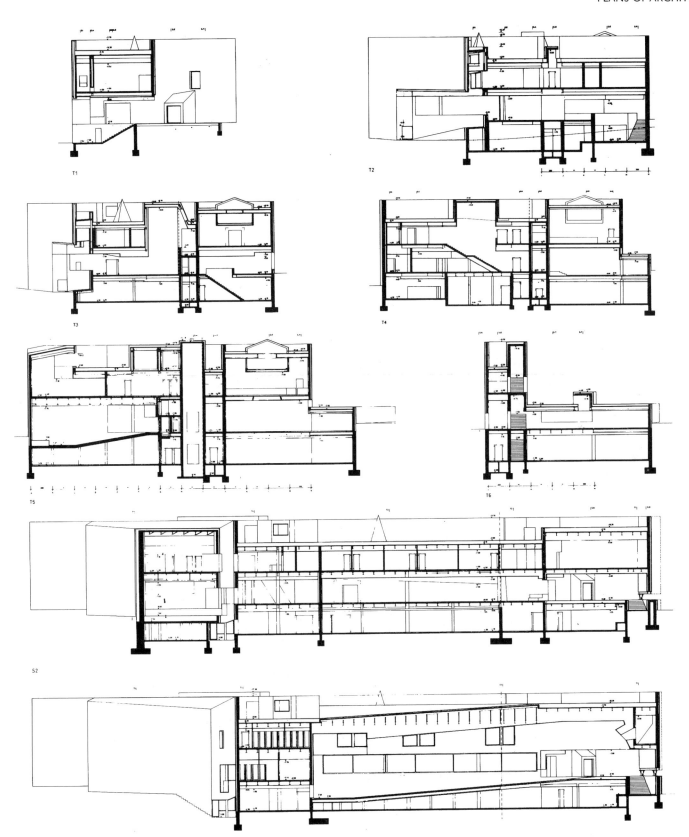

T1

T2

T3

T4

T5

T6

S2

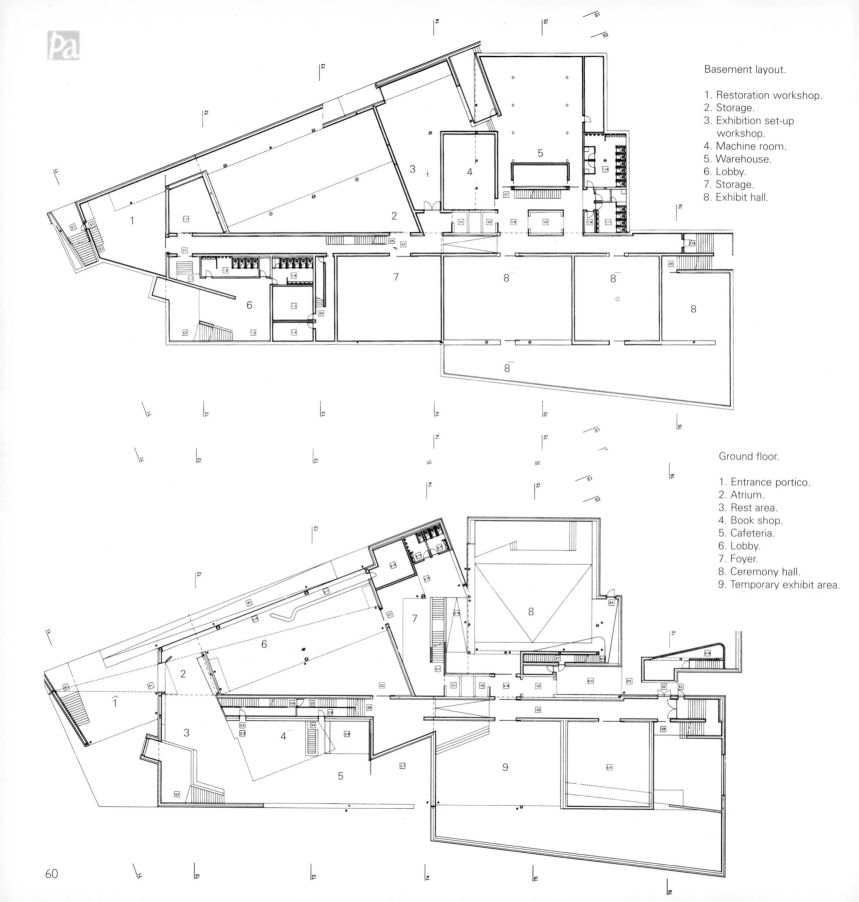

Basement layout.

1. Restoration workshop.
2. Storage.
3. Exhibition set-up workshop.
4. Machine room.
5. Warehouse.
6. Lobby.
7. Storage.
8. Exhibit hall.

Ground floor.

1. Entrance portico.
2. Atrium.
3. Rest area.
4. Book shop.
5. Cafeteria.
6. Lobby.
7. Foyer.
8. Ceremony hall.
9. Temporary exhibit area.

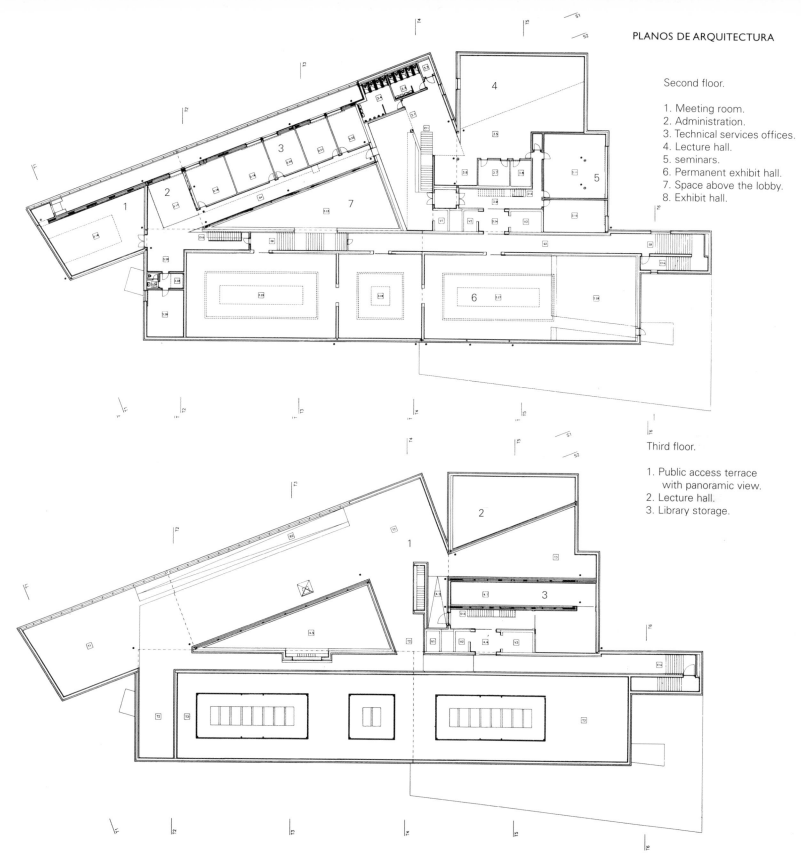

PLANOS DE ARQUITECTURA

Second floor.

1. Meeting room.
2. Administration.
3. Technical services offices.
4. Lecture hall.
5. seminars.
6. Permanent exhibit hall.
7. Space above the lobby.
8. Exhibit hall.

Third floor.

1. Public access terrace
   with panoramic view.
2. Lecture hall.
3. Library storage.

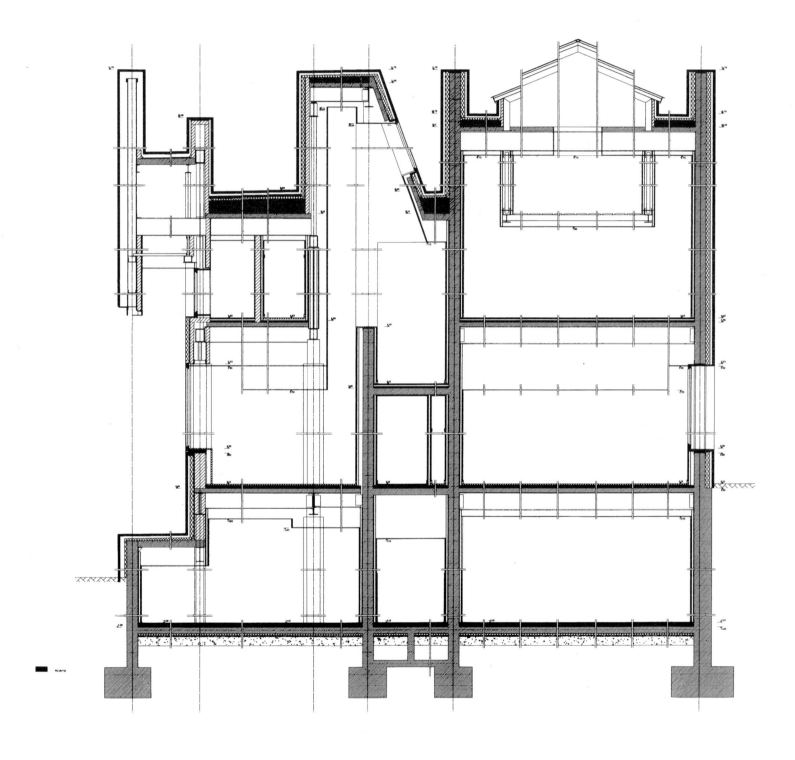

Acero

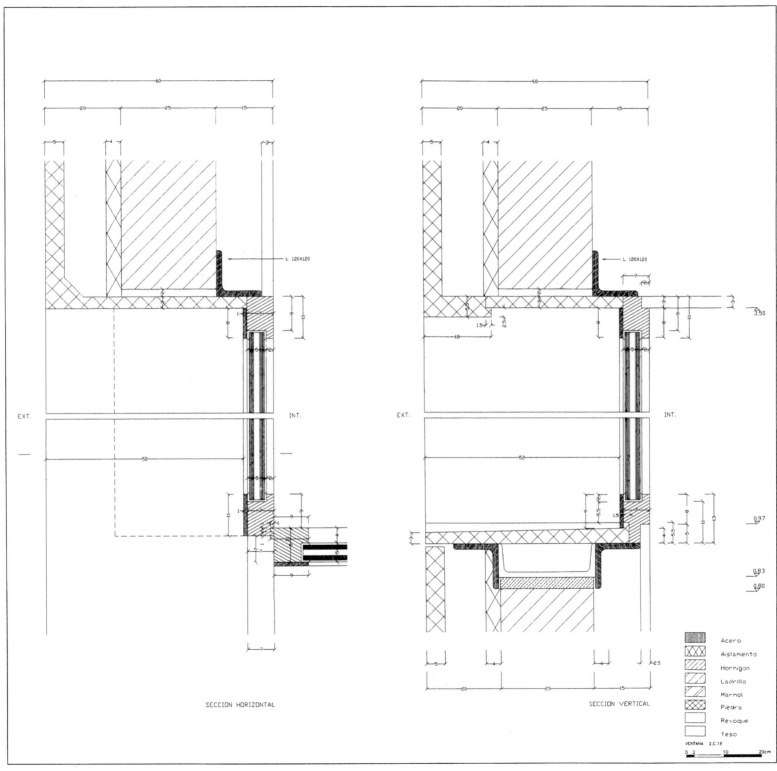

L 120X120

EXT.   INT.

SECCION HORIZONTAL

L 120X120

3.50

EXT.   INT.

0.97

0.83
0.80

SECCION VERTICAL

Acero
Aislamiento
Hormigón
Ladrillo
Marmol
Piedra
Revoque
Yeso

VENTANA 2.C.16

0 2   10   20cm

Vincity plan.

Architect: *Scogin Elam and Bray Architects, Inc.*
Merill Elam and Mack Scogin with Lloyd Bray
Location: *Corning, New York (USA)*
Building Area: *11,000 gross square feet*
Client: *Corning Incorporated*
Structural Engineer: *Pruitt Eberly Stone, Inc.*
Mechanical/Electrical Engineer: *Adams Davis Partners*
Graphic Design: *William S.Lucas, Corning Corporate Architecture and*
Design.
Cost: *$1.2 million*

The architecture of the Corning Child Development Center is derived from two sets of criteria: the program and objectives generated by the adult - the need for functionality, order, safety and any other number of pragmatic criteria; and the child's sensitivities and fantasies that adults can not always quantify. The architectural intention is to transform these "givens" into an environment that peaks the imagination and lifts the spirit of the child as well as the child in the adult.

The center is at once totally rational and serendipitously fanciful. Like building blocks which are measurable and rational in every way, it is the combination of blocks in infinite variety, the relationship of the spaces between and through them, that is greater than the measurable total. Motion implied by the variety of shapes and spaces lends vitality and energy and speaks to the process of children learning through movement.

It is nice to consider that the building could, in some ways, contribute to the child's development of values that will inform and structure his/her adult world. The architecture, in effect, becomes a tool for the imagination.

The program can accommodate up to one hundred and forty-four children, ages six weeks through pre-kindergarten. The program and the building plan are developed on the concept of "family groups" with age-specific classrooms grouped together so that children in a range of ages interact wich each other.

Building construction is slab on grade with an internal heating system wood framing with wood and steel truss joists natural and stained wood siding at the exterior walls insulated glazing in aluminum frames elastomeric membrane roofing, and painted gypsum wall board, carpet, vinyl composition tile, and sealed plywood and painted metal trim on the interior. Common building products and materials are "tweaked" in a variety of ways to respond to the child's point of view.

Ground floor plan. Scale 1:500.

Mezzanine plan. Scale 1:500.

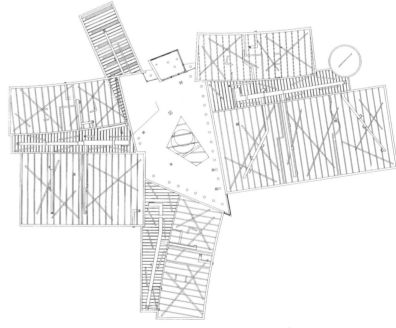

Lighting layout. Scale 1:500.

Reflected ceiling plan. Scale 1:500.

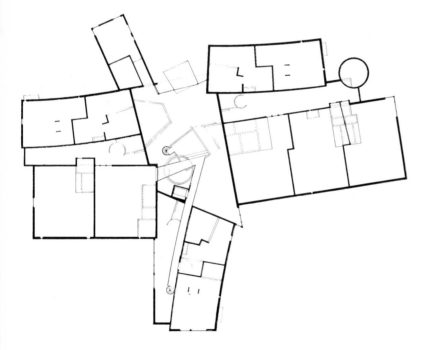

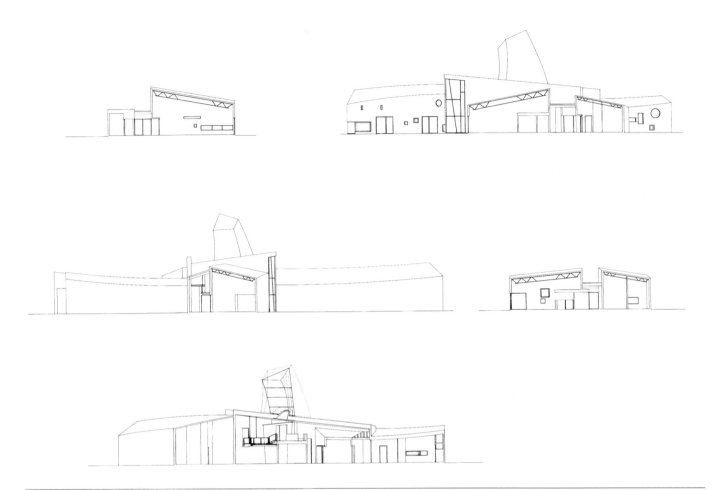

Sections. Scale 1:500.

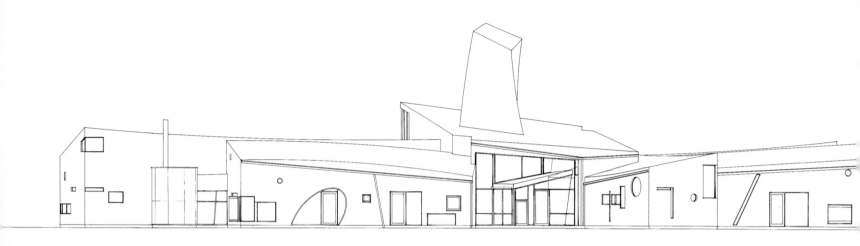

South elevation. Scale 1:200.

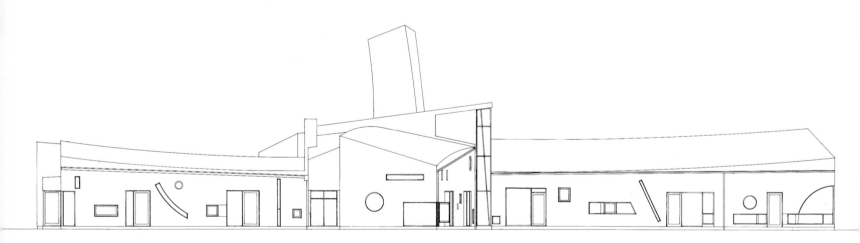

North elevation. Scale 1:200.

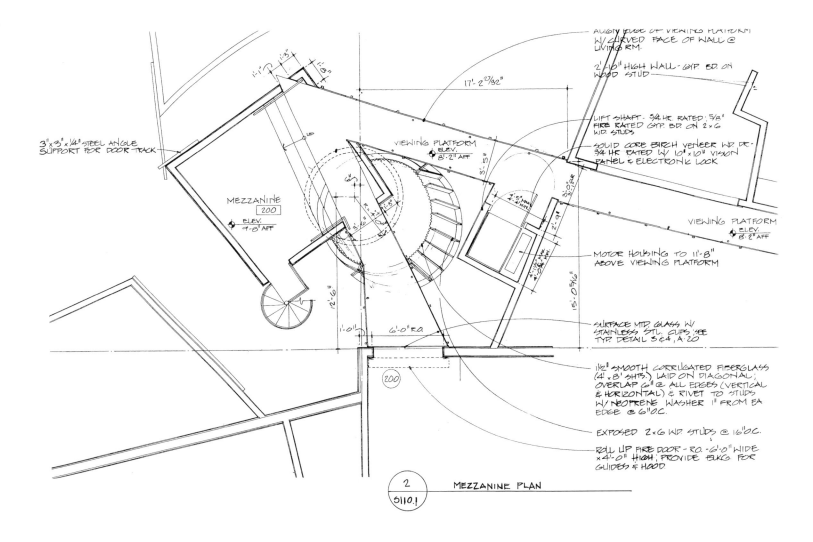

ALIGN EDGE OF VIEWING PLATFORM W/ CURVED FACE OF WALL @ LIVING RM.

2'-10" HIGH WALL - GYP. BD. ON WOOD STUD

LIFT SHAFT - 3/4 HR. RATED; 5/8" FIRE RATED GYP. BD. ON 2×6 WD. STUDS

SOLID CORE BIRCH VENEER WD. DR. - 3/4 HR. RATED W/ 10"×10" VISION PANEL & ELECTRONIC LOCK

3"×3"×1/4" STEEL ANGLE SUPPORT FOR DOOR TRACK

17'- 2 ²³/₃₂"

VIEWING PLATFORM
ELEV.
8'-2" AFF

MEZZANINE
200
ELEV.
9'-8" AFF

VIEWING PLATFORM
ELEV.
8'-2" AFF

MOTOR HOUSING TO 11'-8" ABOVE VIEWING PLATFORM

UP

12'-6"

1'-0"

6'-0" R.O.

200

SURFACE MTD. GLASS W/ STAINLESS STL. CLIPS; SEE TYP. DETAIL 3 & 4, A-20

1½" SMOOTH CORRUGATED FIBERGLASS (4'×8' SHTS.) LAID ON DIAGONAL; OVERLAP 6" @ ALL EDGES (VERTICAL & HORIZONTAL) & RIVET TO STUDS W/ NEOPRENE WASHER 1" FROM EA. EDGE @ 6"O.C.

EXPOSED 2×6 WD. STUDS @ 16"O.C.

ROLL UP FIRE DOOR - R.O. - 6'-0" WIDE ×4'-0" HIGH; PROVIDE BLKG. FOR GUIDES & HOOD.

2
S110.1

MEZZANINE PLAN

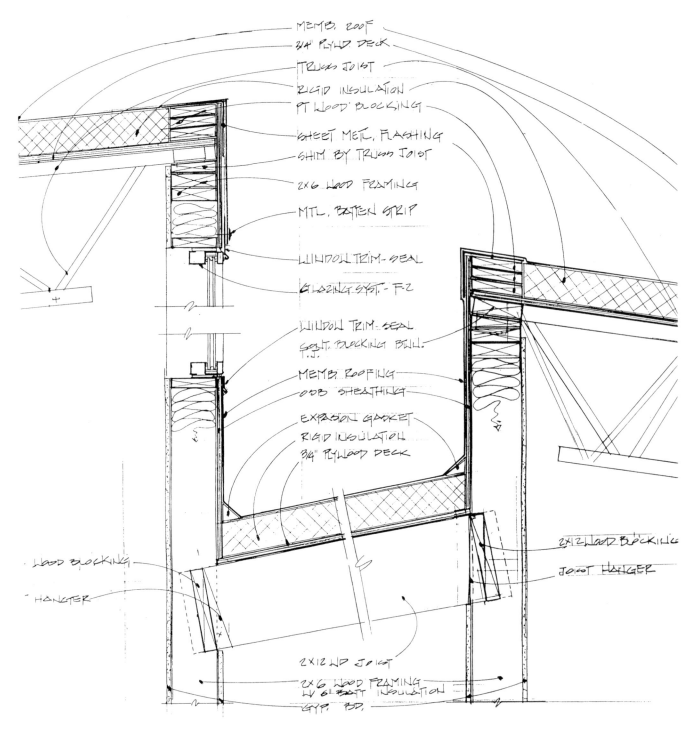

MEMB. ROOF
3/4" PLYWD. DECK
TRUSS JOIST
RIGID INSULATION
PT WOOD BLOCKING
SHEET METL. FLASHING
SHIM BY TRUSS JOIST
2X6 WOOD FRAMING
MTL. BATTEN STRIP
WINDOW TRIM - SEAL
GLAZING SYST. - F-2
WINDOW TRIM - SEAL
CONT. BLOCKING BTWN.
T.J.
MEMB. ROOFING
OSB SHEATHING
EXPANSION GASKET
RIGID INSULATION
3/4" PLYWOOD DECK

2X12 WOOD BLOCKING
JOIST HANGER

WOOD BLOCKING
HANGER

2X12 WD JOIST
2X6 WOOD FRAMING
W/ 6" BATT INSULATION
GYP. BD.

SECTION @ LIVING ROOM
5 1/2" = 1'-0"

72

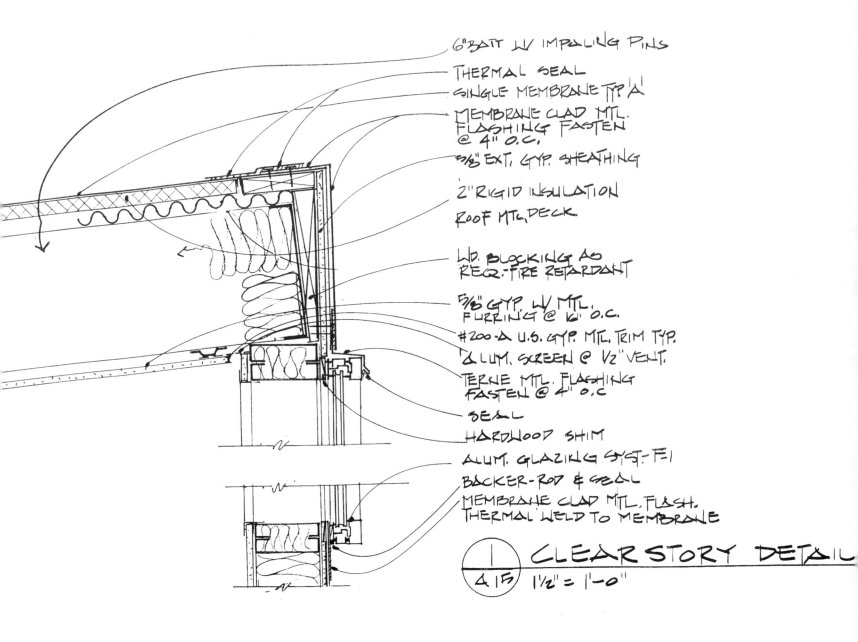

6" BATT W/ IMPALING PINS

THERMAL SEAL

SINGLE MEMBRANE TYP 'A'

MEMBRANE CLAD MTL.
FLASHING FASTEN
@ 4" O.C.

3/8" EXT. GYP. SHEATHING

2" RIGID INSULATION

ROOF MTL. DECK

WD. BLOCKING AS
REQ.- FIRE RETARDANT

5/8" GYP. W/ MTL.
FURRING @ 6" O.C.

#200-A U.S. GYP. MTL. TRIM TYP.

ALUM. SCREEN @ 1/2" VENT.

TERNE MTL. FLASHING
FASTEN @ 4" O.C.

SEAL

HARDWOOD SHIM

ALUM. GLAZING SYST.-F-1

BACKER-ROD & SEAL

MEMBRANE CLAD MTL. FLASH.
THERMAL WELD TO MEMBRANE

① CLEARSTORY DETAIL
A15 1 1/2" = 1'-0"

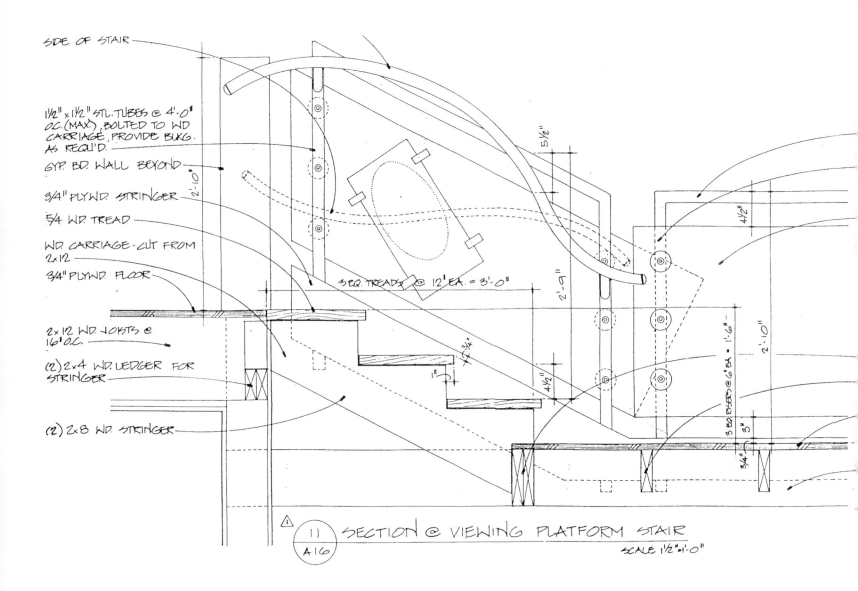

SIDE OF STAIR

1½" x 1½" STL. TUBES @ 4'-0"
O.C. (MAX.), BOLTED TO WD.
CARRIAGE, PROVIDE BLKG.
AS REQU'D.

GYP. BD. WALL BEYOND

¾" PLYWD. STRINGER

5/4 WD. TREAD

WD. CARRIAGE · CUT FROM
2 x 12

¾" PLYWD. FLOOR

2 x 12 WD. JOISTS @
16' O.C.

(2) 2 x 4 WD. LEDGER FOR
STRINGER

(2) 2 x 8 WD. STRINGER

3 EQ. TREADS @ 12' EA. = 3'-0"

△ ⑪ SECTION @ VIEWING PLATFORM STAIR
  A 16   SCALE 1½"=1'-0"

" x 1½" CONT. STL. TUBE TOP
L

" x 1½" STL. TUBES @ 4'-0"
. (MAX.), BOLTED TO WD.
RINGER' W/ 3/8" Ø LAG
LTS, 3½" LONG

4" EDGE BANDED PLYWD.
NELS; ATTACH TO STEEL
BES W/ 3'Ø STAINLESS
EEL WASHERS & BOLTS @
OC. VERT.

) 2 x 8 WD. HEADER

6 WD. JOISTS @ 16" OC.

4" PLYWD. FLOOR

EWING PLATFORM
-2" AFF

) 2 x 8 WD. STRINGER

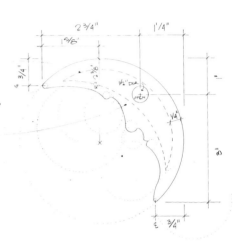

LINE OF 3/4"
PLYWOOD SPACER
BEYOND - PTD.

½" BIRCH PULL
W/ STAIN & CLR
SEALER ATTACHED
TO CAB. DOOR W/
(2) #4 ROUND HD
WOOD SCREWS

2¾" 1¼"
1 5/8"
3/4"
½"DIA.
OPEN
¼"
3"
3/4"

(22 / A24) DOOR PULL B
3/4" = 1"

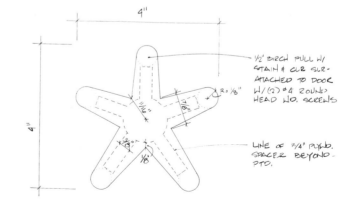

4"

½" BIRCH PULL W/
STAIN & CLR SLR.
ATTACHED TO DOOR
W/ (2) #4 ROUND
HEAD WD. SCREWS

LINE OF 3/4" PLYWD.
SPACER BEYOND -
PTD.

R = 1/8"
1/16"
3/4"
3/8"
1/8"

(23 / A24) DOOR PULL C
3/4" = 1"

NOTE:
FABRICATE 1/3 OF REQUIRED TOTAL
NUMBER OF EACH: 21-A24,
22-A24 & 23-A24

75

Franck Hammoutène

Architect: *Franck Hammoutene.*
Site: *Music City. Paris (France).*
Collaborators: *A. Ferraru, R. Gazzolaa, P. Gerent, S. Pratte, J.L. Rey.*
Project team: *J. Auzolle, A. Ferraru, J. Montfort, F. Rabiet.*
Engineering: *GET Ingenierie, ALTO Ingenierie.*
Area: *418 square feet.*

The Music Museum lies between park and city in the east part of Music City. In 1990, a contest took place which awarded Frank Hammoutene the project of designing the exhibition halls (permanent and temporary) and all of the designing connected with displaying and arranging the exhibits inside the volumes previously created by Christian de Portzamparc.

The museum's objective is to contribute to musical knowledge and to the conservation of the musical heritage, thereby presenting instrumental and iconographic collections such as sculpture, paintings and architecture which offer testimony to music in every aspect. Music is here represented through everything which brings it to life, from instruments and scores to the orchestra and even to music hall architecture. For the conception of such a museum it was necessary to invent a new architecture within an already existing space, albeit one intended for other ends.

The project came with the necessity of sculpting a suitable setting for each of nine sections depicting important musical events - revolutions, doubts, discoveries, new or consecrated methods. Each section focuses on a major work illustrated by an instrumental arrangement next to a sketch of the place of its creation. For example, the hall of the Ducal Palace in Mantua where Claudio Monteverdi composed Orpheon and The Elysium Fields Theater where Igor Stravinsky wrote his Ode to Spring.

The project is a series of merged cadences, measures, rhythms and passages - a refuge from the city where rigidity dominates. Here, wood, waxed concrete and gray gives priority to the materials and colors of the instruments.

The display of the collections is unusually dense (arranged linearly as imposed by the shape of the buildings) and therefore creates an intimate relationship between visitor and work and calls to mind a "private collection" much more than a "public institutional museum". Thus, an architectural walkway is developed on eight levels where each discovery leads to the next in alternating prolongations of space like a continuous musical verse.

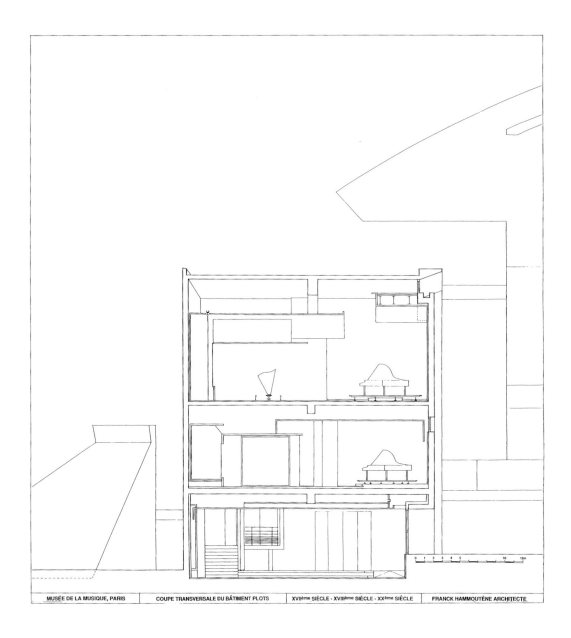

| MUSÉE DE LA MUSIQUE, PARIS | COUPE TRANSVERSALE DU BÂTIMENT PLOTS | XVIIème SIÈCLE - XVIIIème SIÈCLE - XXème SIÈCLE | FRANCK HAMMOUTÈNE ARCHITECTE |

Cross section of the building containing the seventeenth, eighteenth and nineteenth century collections.

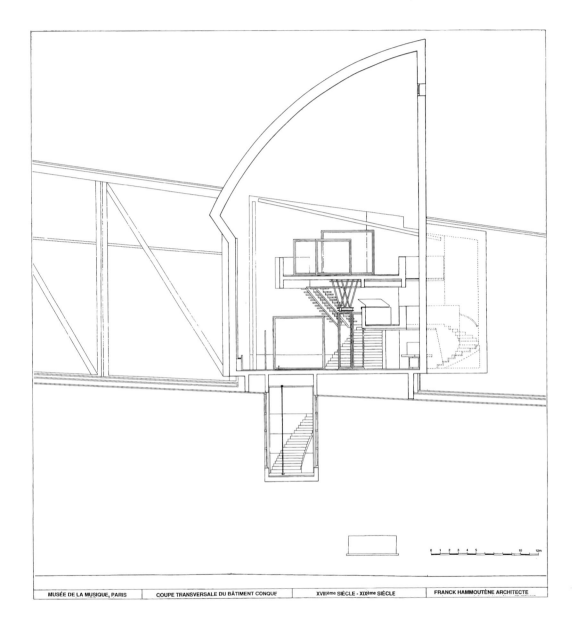

| MUSÉE DE LA MUSIQUE, PARIS | COUPE TRANSVERSALE DU BÂTIMENT CONQUE | XVIIIème SIÈCLE - XIXème SIÈCLE | FRANCK HAMMOUTÈNE ARCHITECTE |

Cross section of the building containing the twentieth century collection.

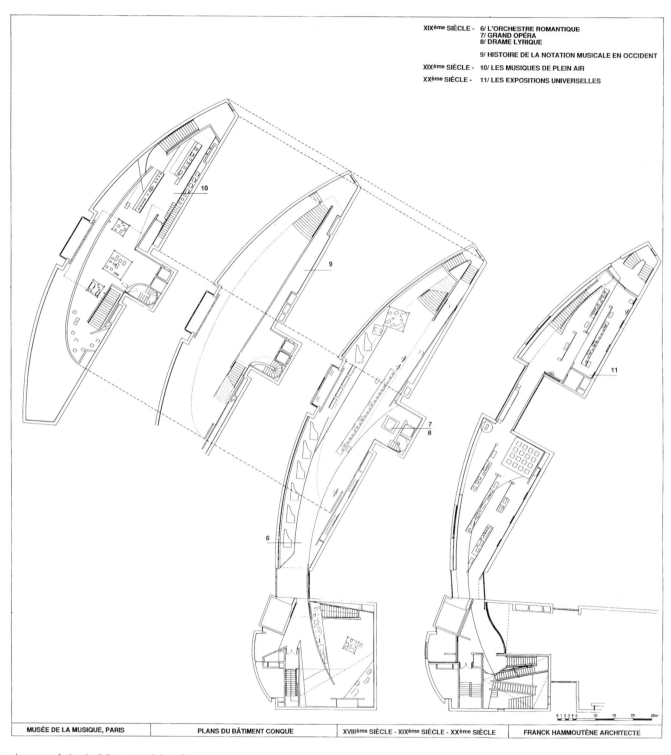

XIXème SIÈCLE - 6/ L'ORCHESTRE ROMANTIQUE
7/ GRAND OPÉRA
8/ DRAME LYRIQUE

9/ HISTOIRE DE LA NOTATION MUSICALE EN OCCIDENT
XIXème SIÈCLE - 10/ LES MUSIQUES DE PLEIN AIR
XXème SIÈCLE - 11/ LES EXPOSITIONS UNIVERSELLES

| MUSÉE DE LA MUSIQUE, PARIS | PLANS DU BÂTIMENT CONQUE | XVIIIème SIÈCLE - XIXème SIÈCLE - XXème SIÈCLE | FRANCK HAMMOUTÈNE ARCHITECTE |

Layout of the building containing the seventeenth, eighteenth and nineteenth century collections.

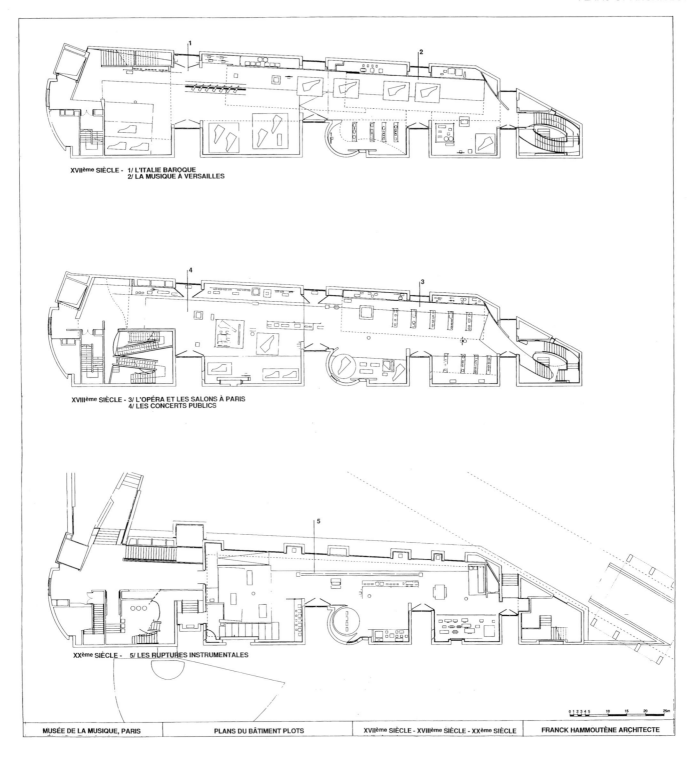

XVIIème SIÈCLE - 1/ L'ITALIE BAROQUE
2/ LA MUSIQUE À VERSAILLES

XVIIIème SIÈCLE - 3/ L'OPÉRA ET LES SALONS À PARIS
4/ LES CONCERTS PUBLICS

XXème SIÈCLE - 5/ LES RUPTURES INSTRUMENTALES

| MUSÉE DE LA MUSIQUE, PARIS | PLANS DU BÂTIMENT PLOTS | XVIIème SIÈCLE - XVIIIème SIÈCLE - XXème SIÈCLE | FRANCK HAMMOUTÈNE ARCHITECTE |

Layout of the building containing the twentieth century collection.

Vertical section of a display
case. Scale 1:4

FIXATION EN PLANCHER HAUT GROS OEUVRE PAR CHEVILLES ET

ÉTRIER ACI

RÉGLAGE VERTICAL BOULON PERCÉ ET CONTRE-ÉCF

CÂBLE INOX ⌀ 4 m

CALE DE BLOCAGE DU BALAN TRANSVERSAL DU VITRAG

FIBRE OPTIQU

COLLAGE V.E.C. SILICONE BI-COMPOSANT

RÉGLAGE ÉCARTEURS

COQUE ACIER TOUTE LONGUEUR (RÉPARTITION DES CHARGES) EN DEU;
PARTIES BOULONNÉES

TUBE ALUMINIUM POUR COLLAGE V.E.C. AVEC ANODISATION SPÉCIFIQUE

PLAT DE REHAUSSE

INSERT FIBRE OPTIQUE EN ALUMINIUM MOULÉ

ÉTANCHÉITÉ JOINT BALAI CONTRE BANDE AUTOCOLLANTE

RACCORD PLAFOND/VITRINE

VITRAGE SUSPENDU FEUILLETÉ RECUIT 66/2

PARQUET DENSIFIÉ HÊTRE OU FRÊNE VERNIS MAT

CHAPE DE FINITION POUR POSE PARQUET OU TRAITÉE APPARENTE
SELON LOCALISATION

COUCHE RÉSILIENTE DEUX NAPPES ASSOUR-V À RECOUVREMENT

DALLE BÉTON ARMÉ STRUCTURELLE

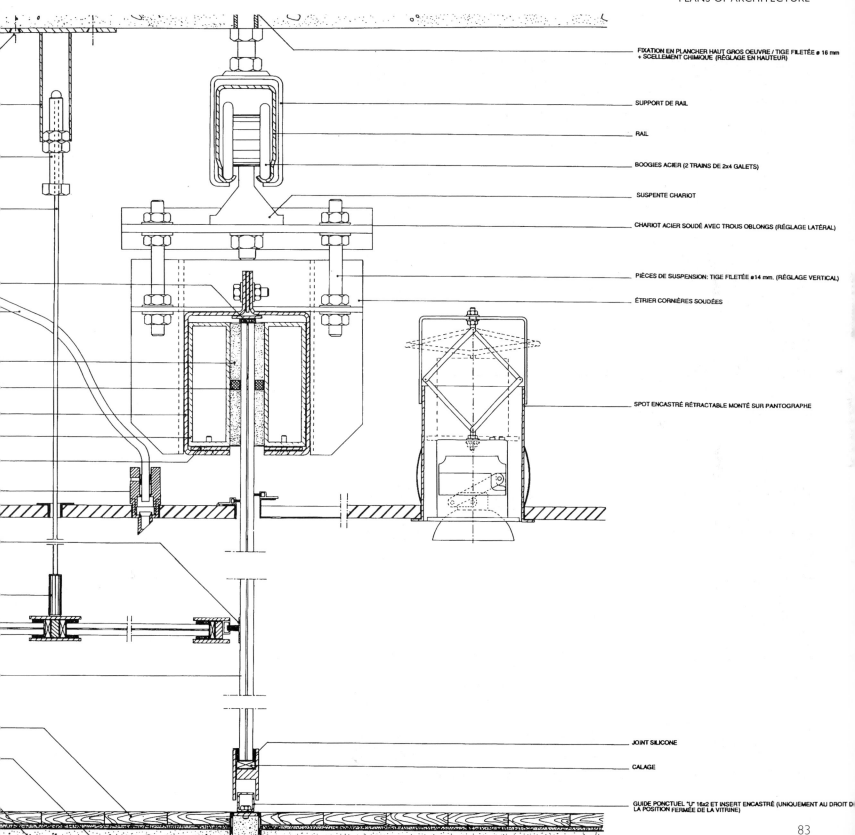

FIXATION EN PLANCHER HAUT GROS OEUVRE / TIGE FILETÉE ø 16 mm + SCELLEMENT CHIMIQUE (RÉGLAGE EN HAUTEUR)

SUPPORT DE RAIL

RAIL

BOOGIES ACIER (2 TRAINS DE 2x4 GALETS)

SUSPENTE CHARIOT

CHARIOT ACIER SOUDÉ AVEC TROUS OBLONGS (RÉGLAGE LATÉRAL)

PIÉCES DE SUSPENSION: TIGE FILETÉE ø14 mm. (RÉGLAGE VERTICAL)

ÉTRIER CORNIÈRES SOUDÉES

SPOT ENCASTRÉ RÉTRACTABLE MONTÉ SUR PANTOGRAPHE

JOINT SILICONE

CALAGE

GUIDE PONCTUEL "U" 16x2 ET INSERT ENCASTRÉ (UNIQUEMENT AU DROIT D LA POSITION FERMÉE DE LA VITRINE)

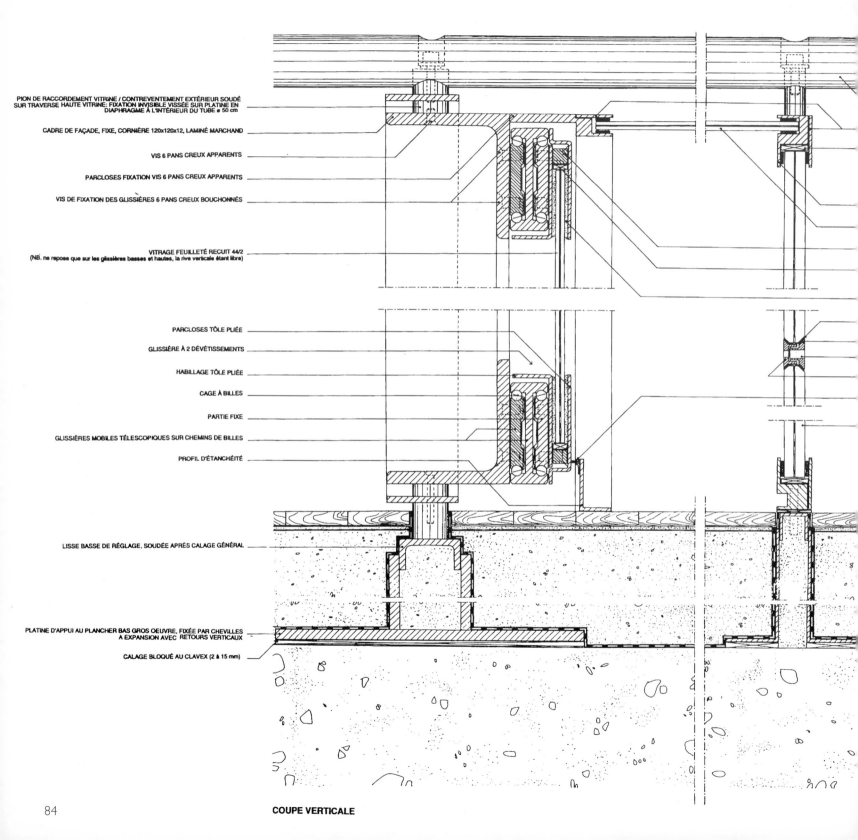

PION DE RACCORDEMENT VITRINE / CONTREVENTEMENT EXTÉRIEUR SOUDÉ
SUR TRAVERSE HAUTE VITRINE: FIXATION INVISIBLE VISSÉE SUR PLATINE EN
DIAPHRAGME À L'INTÉRIEUR DU TUBE Ø 50 cm

CADRE DE FAÇADE, FIXE, CORNIÈRE 120x120x12, LAMINÉ MARCHAND

VIS 6 PANS CREUX APPARENTS

PARCLOSES FIXATION VIS 6 PANS CREUX APPARENTS

VIS DE FIXATION DES GLISSIÈRES 6 PANS CREUX BOUCHONNÉS

VITRAGE FEUILLETÉ RECUIT 44/2
(NB. ne repose que sur les glissières basses et hautes, la rive verticale étant libre)

PARCLOSES TÔLE PLIÉE

GLISSIÈRE À 2 DÉVÊTISSEMENTS

HABILLAGE TÔLE PLIÉE

CAGE À BILLES

PARTIE FIXE

GLISSIÈRES MOBILES TÉLESCOPIQUES SUR CHEMINS DE BILLES

PROFIL D'ÉTANCHÉITÉ

LISSE BASSE DE RÉGLAGE, SOUDÉE APRÈS CALAGE GÉNÉRAL

PLATINE D'APPUI AU PLANCHER BAS GROS OEUVRE, FIXÉE PAR CHEVILLES
A EXPANSION AVEC RETOURS VERTICAUX

CALAGE BLOQUÉ AU CLAVEX (2 à 15 mm)

COUPE VERTICALE

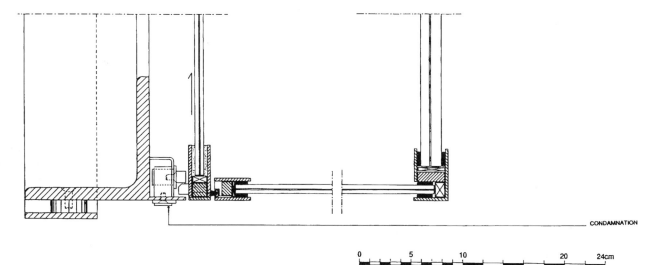

Detail. Scale 1:4.

TUBE ELECTROSOUDÉ ⌀ 50 cm CONTREVENTE

PARCLOSES FIXATION VIS 6 PANS CREUX APP.

CALAGE

PROFIL DE RIVE ARRIÈRE

VITRAGE FEUILLETÉ RECUIT 44/2

ESPACEUR (FIXATION INVISIBLE DU PARCLOSA
BOUCHONNÉS

CALAGE

JOINT SILICONE

INTERFACE BAGUE NYLON

INSERT INOX FACE EXTERNE

FILETAGE INTÉRIEUR POUR FIXATION DES SUP

INSERT INOX FACE INTERNE

JOINT BALAI

VITRAGE FEUILLETÉ RECUIT 10.10.2

PARQUET DENSIFIÉ HÊTRE OU FRÊNE VERNIS

CHAPE DE FINITION POUR POSE PARQUET OU
SELON LOCALISATION

COUCHE RÉSILILNTE DEUX NAPPES ASSOUR-V

DALLE STRUCTURELLE

CONDAMNATION

0   5   10   20   24cm

Architects: Günter Behnisch, Winfried Buxel, Manfred Sabatke.
Site: Bonn. Germany
Client: Bundestag
Project architects: G.Starb, H.Burkart, E.Pritzer, A.Salmuth, E. Tillmanns.
Structural design: Schlaich, Bergermannn and Partner
Landscape design: Hans Luz + Partner

The Parliament occupies a privileged location on the banks of the Rhine close to a long riverside walk. In view of the considerable size of the building, one of the aims of the design was to keep its impact on the landscape to a minimum.

Behnisch has established connections between the architecture and the natural surroundings by way of subtle insinuations and references: a stairway resembles a bird's nest; continuity is established between a path outside the building and an interior trajectory and so on.

The roof is practically transparent. Crowned by a skylight, the room is transformed into a small valley in a forest, a place where light filters through the branches of the trees. The presence of the natural world is constant inside the building: day and night, sunrise and sunset, winter snows, the leaden colour of the autumn sky, the colour of spring flowers. The laws and decisions that affect the whole country are made in a place which is very similar to the one where the inhabitants of the area, today known as Germany, once gathered together: a clearing in the forest.

Obviously, the implementation of this metaphor required enormous technical effort, not only owing to problems relating to climatic conditions and interior temperature, but also because of security needs. In the event, some aspects of the project had to be modified owing to these restraints.

Even so, the idea of transparency has been maintained. It is still possible to see right through the building: the trees are visible from the Parliamentary chamber; the Representatives gallery can be seen from the lobby; and there is a view of the river from the stairs. The images are layered, superimposed on one another. The walls have been de-materialised so that we can see what is happening behind them.

There are two entrances to the lobby from the square: one on the right for Representatives, and one on the left for visitors.

Entering by the right hand door, the Representatives descend a wide staircase to the lobby, where there is a door into the Parliamentary Chamber. A broad walkway on the entrance level leads to the offices of the President of the Chamber. People using the visitor's entrance can either go down to the conference room or up to the viewing gallery. The Parliamentary Chamber is surrounded by antechambers or side lobbies that afford views of the exterior as well as of the Chamber itself. Following an age old tradition, it is here in the antechambers that off-the-record conversations take place. There is a third entrance on the riverfront façade which is used on ceremonial occasions. A wide stairway leads up from the riverside to a platform in front of the building. welcoming or saying goodbye to important guests.

The building is not only transparent to the eyes, but also to movement. There is continuity, and the spaces are fluid and open, at least as far as security permits.

Behnisch's parliament has been shown to function extremely well in the short time since its opening. However, even less time remains before the relocation of the German Parliament to the old Reichstag building in Berlin.

Site plan. Scale: 1/2500

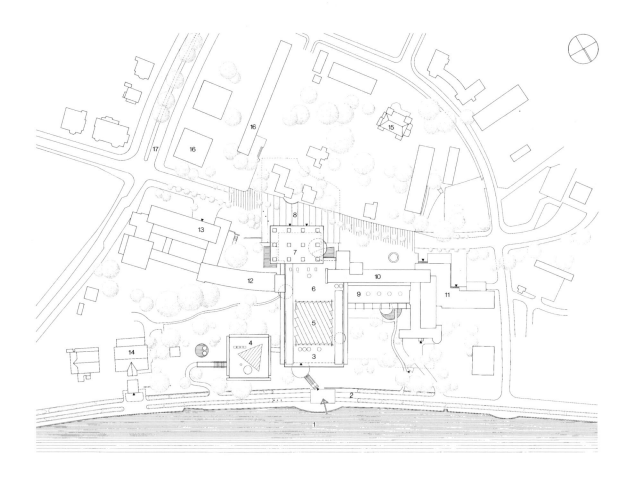

1. Rhine.
2. Embankment.
3. Presidential wing.
4. Presidential annex.
5. Debating chamber.
6. Lobby.
7. Entrance hall.
8. Parliament Square.
9. Restaurant.
10. Pre-existing building.
11. Federal Council.
12. South wing.
13. Old House of Representatives.
14. Water supply.
15. Parliament.
16. Representatives' residence.
17. Heuss Avenue.

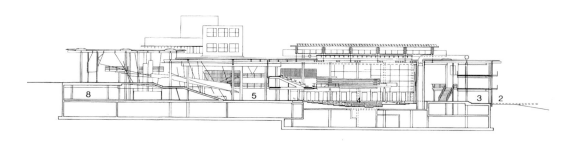

Section. Scale: 1/1000

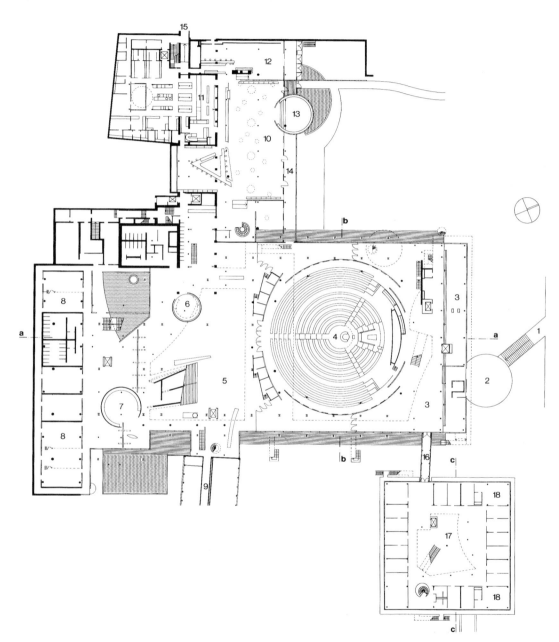

Layout. Scale:1/1000

1. Presidential entrance.
2. Reception terrace.
3. Presidential wing.
4. Plenary hall.
5. Lobby.
6. Information desk.
7. Lounge.
8. Visitor's room.
9. South wing entrance.
10. Restaurant.
11. Kitchen and services.
12. Club.
13. Circular hall.
14. Winter garden.
15. Federal Council entrance.
16. Presidential annex entrance.
17. Lobby.
18. Vice-presidency.

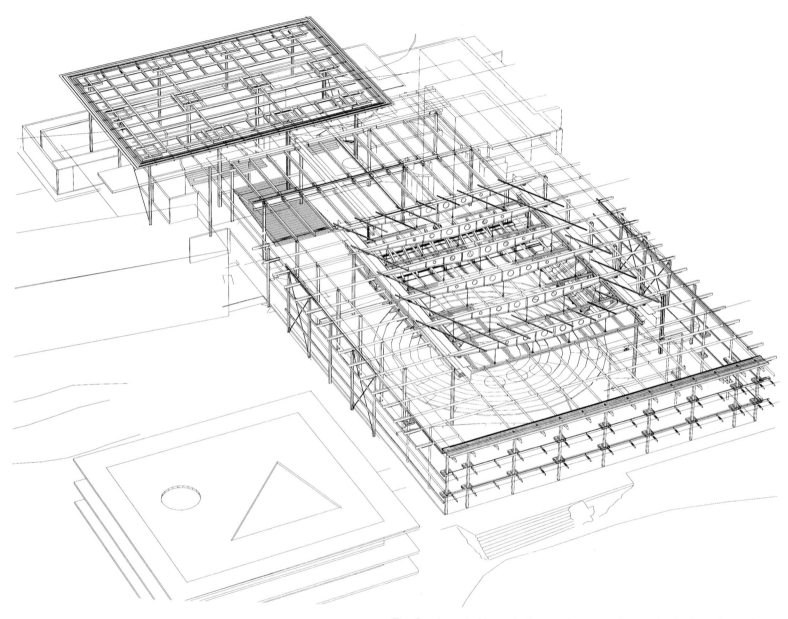

The Bundestag's history is long and plagued with indecision. First, there was an urban contest in which Behnisch's team participated. Then in 1973, there was another for the construction of the building. At that time the objective was to enlarge the already existing building in order to make room for new administrative installations, a plan which subse- quently evolved through various changes and new contests. In 1983 Behnisch was commissioned to do a preliminary sketch of a square in front of the building. This study, however, showed the unfeasibility of adapting the old structure to present needs, which finally led to the decision to knock down the old building and start a new on the same site.

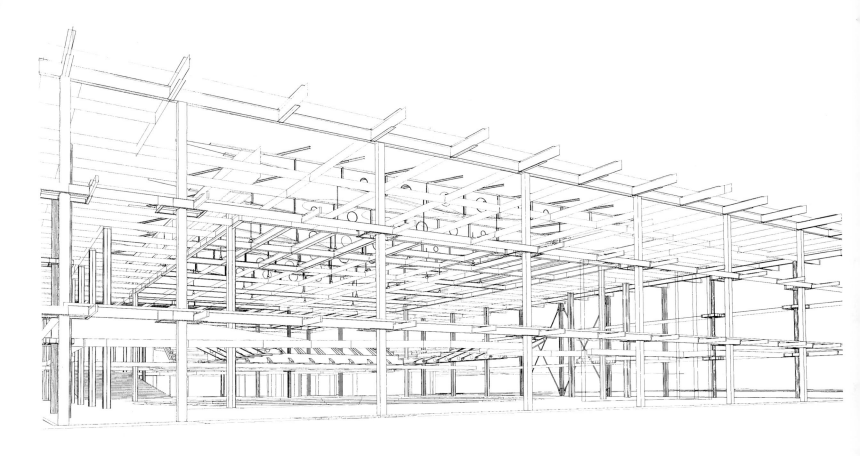

Two axonometric projections of construction of the plenary session hall.

Pillar detail. Scale: 1/50

1. 290 x 290 X 38 mm. welded pillar.
2. C 240 mm. profile edge.
3. 20 mm. steel plate.
4. Circular pillar of 508 X 30 mm. dia.
5. HE-B 450 corbel.
6. HE-M 360 corbel.
7. 50 mm. wallboard.
8. 50 mm. rib.

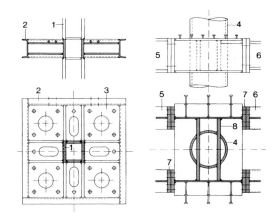

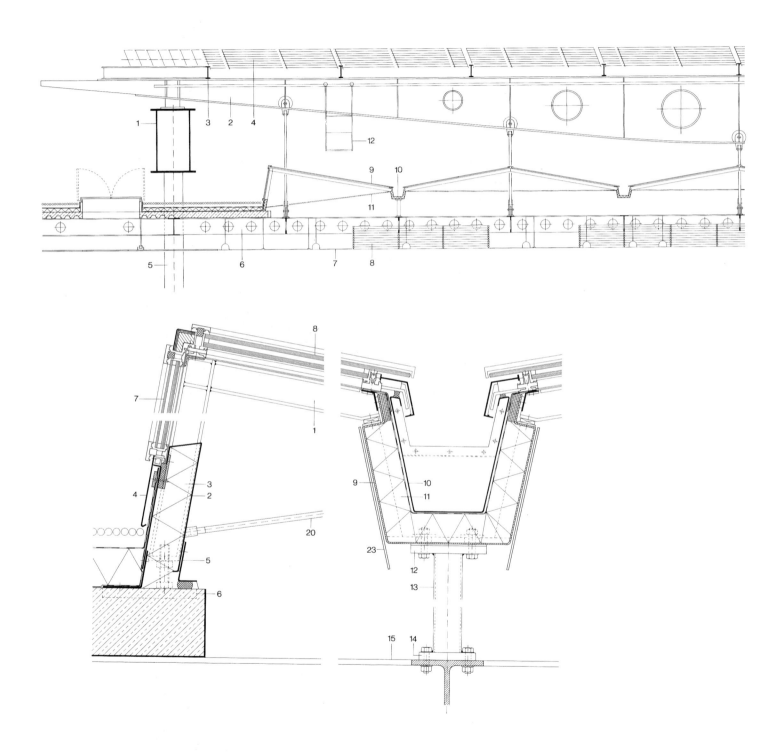

Roof construction scale 1/100

1. Principal beam: 1200 x 1700 mm.
   welded box girder.
2. Fish-belly girders 550 mm.
   flange width.
3. 110 x 300 mm prismatic beams:
   welded sheet metal sections laid
   on diagonal.
4. Adjustable, light-diffusing acrylic
   sheet louvres.
5. Main steel stanchion supporting
   roof light construction: 508 x 40 mm.
6. Framed grid of rolled steel joists.
7. Aluminum panel.
8. Reflecting metal and prismatic
   cast-glass soffit-grid.
9. Folded glass roof light on IPE 80
   beams.
10. Stainless steel box gutter.
11. 16mm tie rods.
12. Travelling maintenance trolley .

Roof light abutments and gutter details 1/10

1. IPE 80 beam.
2. 3mm steel sheet lining.
3. 90 mm foam glass.
4. 3mm aluminum sheet.
5. 103.5 x 50 x 3 mm steel angle.
6. 300 x 250 x 20mm anchor plate.
7. 24 mm laminated safety glass.
8. 33 mm laminated safety glass.
9. 4 mm steel gutter profile.
10. 2 mm stainless steel gutter lining.
11. 73 mm foam glass.
12. D200x20 mm head plate.
13. Steel tube D 76,1 mm.
14. 150 x 260 x 20 mm base plate.
15. Steel framed grid consisting of rolled steel
    joists 450 mm deep.

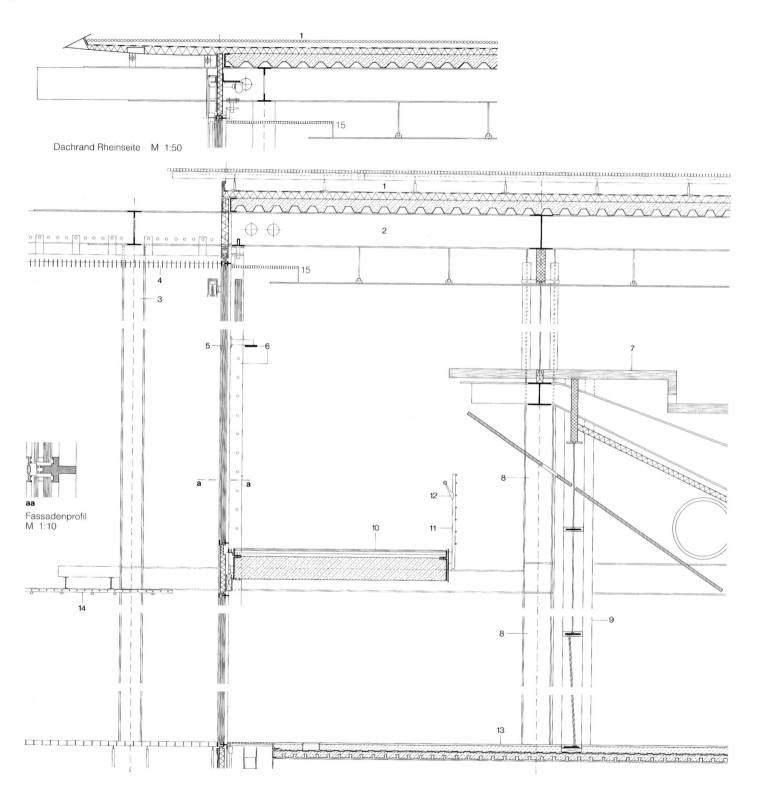

Dachrand Rheinseite   M 1:50

aa
Fassadenprofil
M 1:10

Construction details of the facade.
Plenum building, northeast wing.
Scale:1/50.

1. Roof.
   Fine gravel.
   Asphalt.
   100 mm. insulation.
   100 mm. concrete hollow
   floor filler.
   80 mm. Fretted plate.
2. Lattice of laminated profiles.
   HE-B 450.
3. 300 X 350 mm. concrete-filled
   double core metal pillar.
4. Aluminum solar protection slats.
5. Exterior enclosure.
   Steel profiles with
   aluminum cladding.
   42. mm. insulating safety
   glass with solar protection.
6. 160 x 25 mm. vertical and
   horizontal transom.
7. Tribunal.
   120 mm. laminated wood steps.
   2.40 m. conical profile
   steel beams.
   Insulating ceiling.
   Ventilation tube.
   34 1/2 inclined soffit.
8. 383 X 450 mm. concrete-filled
   double core metal pillar.
9. Hall enclosure.
   260 X 60 mm. horizontal profiles.
   Wood with steel core.
   28 mm. white safety glass.
   120 X 60 mm. double laminated
   wood pillars.
10. Presidential walkway.
    22 mm. parquet.
    30 mm. asphalt sheet.
    48 mm. leveling layer.
    300 mm. concrete sheet.
11. Handrail.
    42.4 X 14.7 mm. vertical transom.
    16 mm. horizontal bars.
12. Cast steel handrail.
13. Floor.
    20 mm. terrazzo.
    80 mm. joist.
    PE sheet.
    Concrete over 80 mm. fretted plate.
    Ventilation duct.
14. Pergola.
15. Iron plate.

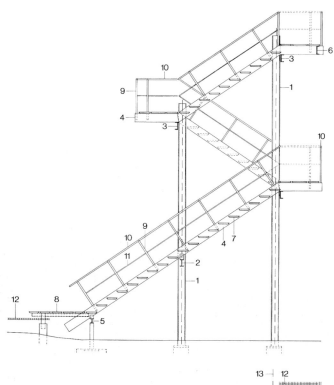

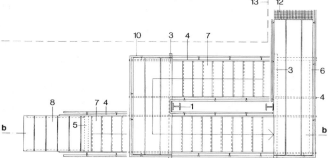

Stairway detail.
Plenum building, notheast corner.
Scale 1:100

1. HEM 180 Pillar.
2. IPE 80 Beam.
3. 200 X 80 mm. profile.
4. 240 X 30 mm. steel plate.
5. HEB 140 beam.
7. 240 X 80 mm. profile.
7. 300 X 40 mm. aluminum profile steps.
8. 400 X 40 mm. aluminum profile plate.
9. 33.7 X 5.6 mm. handrail stud.
10. 3.7 X 5.6 mm. handrail.
11. 16 mm. bar.
12. Steel
13. Facade axis.

Cy Twombly Annex

Renzo Piano

Architect: *Renzo Piano Building Workshop*
Site: *Houston. USA*
Design Team: *S.Ishida, M.Carroll, M.Palmore*
Collaborators: *S.Conner, A.Ewing, S.Lopez, M.Bassignanai (maquetas) y*
R.Fitzgerald & Associates (arquitecto local).
Structure: *Ove Arup & Partners, Londres.*
Engineering: *Haynes Whaley Associates Inc.*
Civil Engineering: *Lockwood, Andrews & Newman*
Construction: *Miner Dederick associates.*

In 1981, Dominique de Menil commissioned Renzo Piano, co-designer of the Pompidou Center in Paris together with Richard Rogers, with the design of the new building for her collection of sur-realistic and primitive African art, which is one of the most important in the world. The site for the museum was a residential area in Houston, comprising small, wood bungalows built in the 19th century.

Five years after the main building was opened, Dominique de Menil charged Renzo Piano with the design of a small exhibition space measuring approximately 9,000 square feet as an annex to the museum, devoted to the works of the American abstract, expressionist artist Cy Twombly.

The appearance of this building is different to that of the main building, according to the express wishes of both the owner and the architect. Nevertheless, they share the same concern: lighting. Working together with Ove Arup, lighting studies were carried out at the Faculty of Architecture and Town Planning at Michigan University. A model of the building was situated under a large, spherical mirror and, via a complex system of computer-controlled lamps, the movement and inten-sity of the Houston sun was reproduced in order to study its effects on the building's interior. The purpose of these studies was to assess the potential of a roof formed by a series of successive fil-ters which would reduce the light's intensity to suitable levels, without concealing its ever-chang-ing nature.

As if to counterbalance the complexity of the roof, the floor layout is simplicity itself: the exhi-bition area is a perfect square, divided into nine equal squares, one for each room.

Unlike the transparent roof, the perimetral walls admit virtually no light, except for the entrance and its opposite in the rear facade. The lack of windows frees the entire wall space for hanging paintings while preventing any reflections.

Sketch.

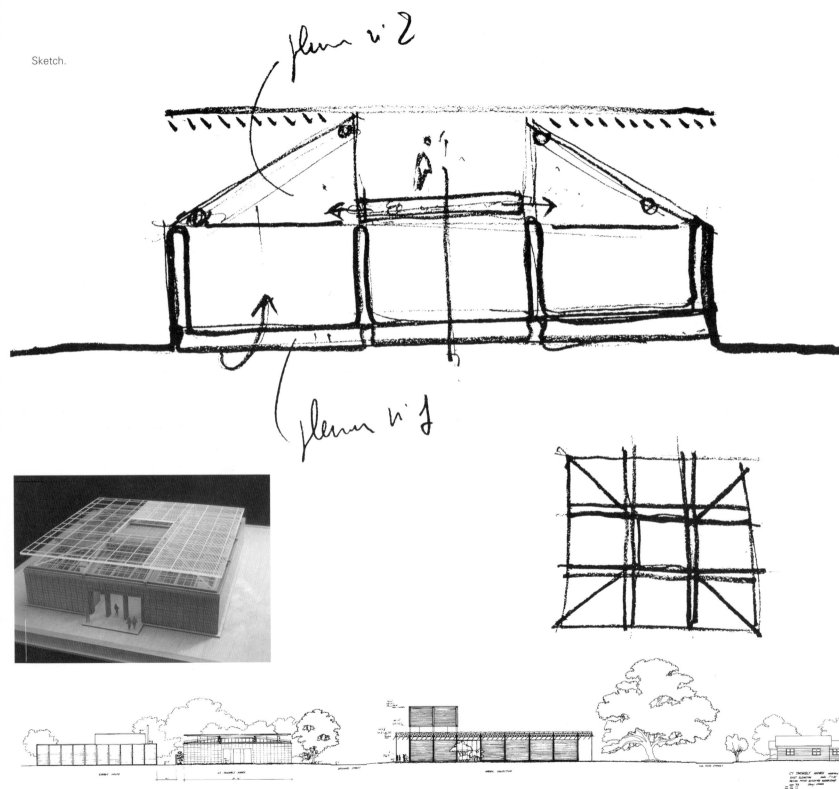

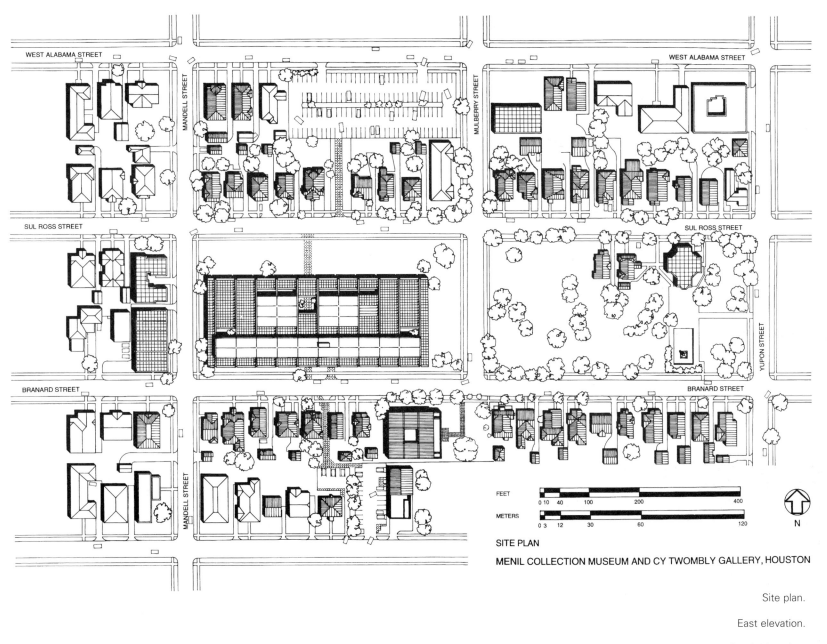

WEST ALABAMA STREET

MANDELL STREET

MULBERRY STREET

WEST ALABAMA STREET

SUL ROSS STREET

SUL ROSS STREET

YUPON STREET

BRANARD STREET

MANDELL STREET

BRANARD STREET

FEET
0 10 40   100   200   400

METERS
0 3 12   30   60   120

N

SITE PLAN

MENIL COLLECTION MUSEUM AND CY TWOMBLY GALLERY, HOUSTON

Site plan.

East elevation.

South elevation.

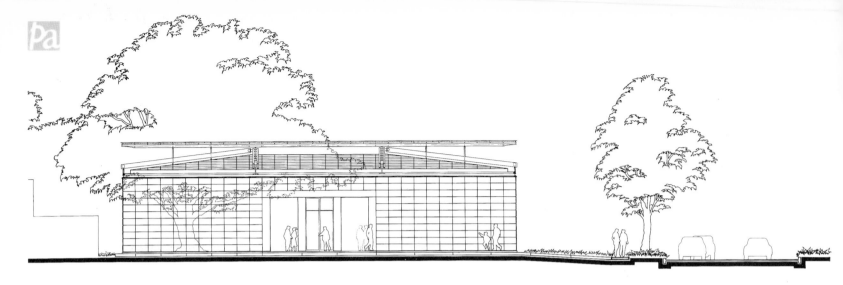

East elevation.

Canopy plan.

EAST ELEVATION

CY TWOMBLY GALLERY
MENIL COLLECTION
HOUSTON, TEXAS

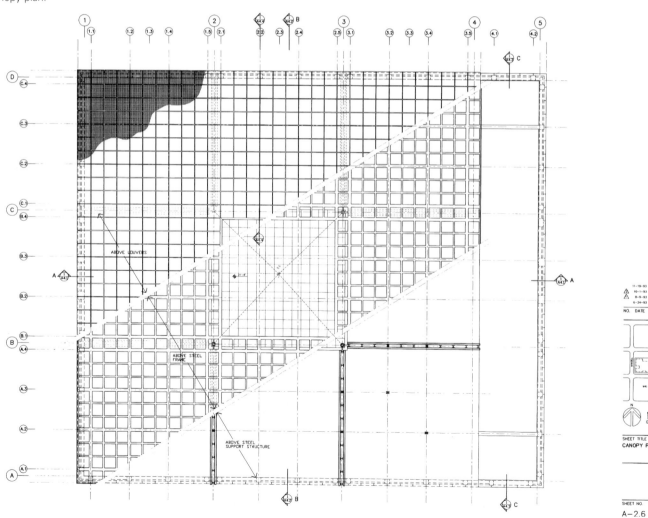

ABOVE LOUVERS

ABOVE STEEL FRAME

ABOVE STEEL SUPPORT STRUCTURE

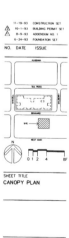

NO.	DATE	ISSUE
	11-19-93	CONSTRUCTION SET
	10-1-93	BUILDING PERMIT SET
	8-9-93	ADDENDUM NO. 1
	6-24-93	FOUNDATION SET

SHEET TITLE
CANOPY PLAN

SHEET NO.
A-2.6

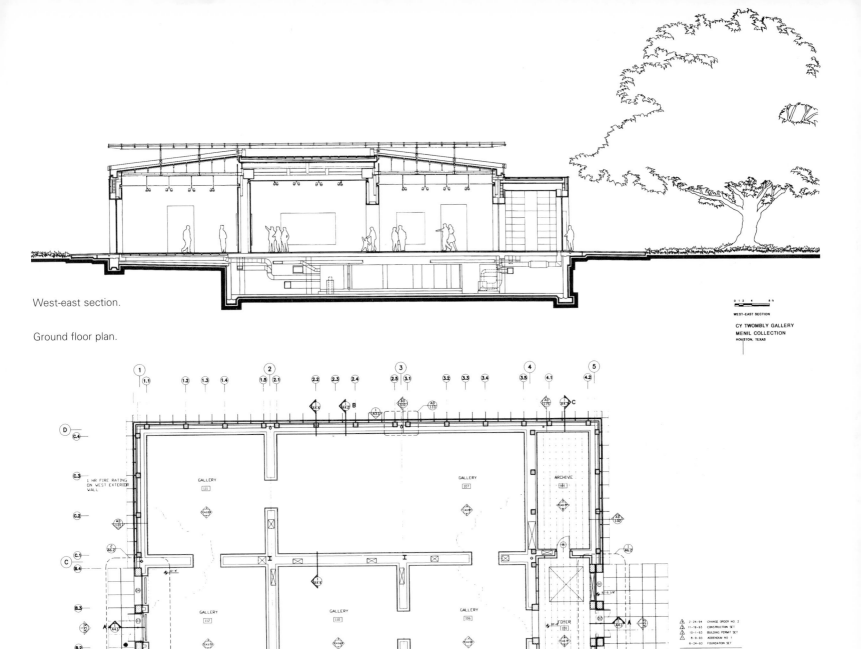

West-east section.

Ground floor plan.

WEST-EAST SECTION

CY TWOMBLY GALLERY
MENIL COLLECTION
HOUSTON, TEXAS

GALLERY

GALLERY

ARCHIVE

1 HR FIRE RATING
ON WEST EXTERIOR
WALL

GALLERY

GALLERY

GALLERY

FOYER

GALLERY

GALLERY

GALLERY

ALCOVE

JAN
CLOSET

MEN'S
HP TOILET
RM

WOMEN'S
HP TOILET
RM

SYMBOLS

SHEET TITLE
GROUND FLOOR PLAN

SHEET NO.
A—2.2

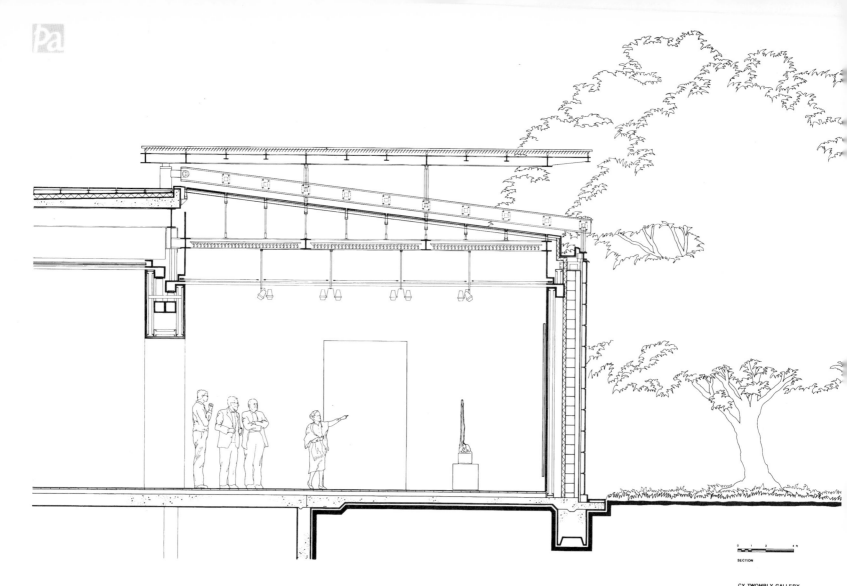

CY TWOMBLY GALLERY
MENIL COLLECTION
HOUSTON, TEXAS

Section detail.

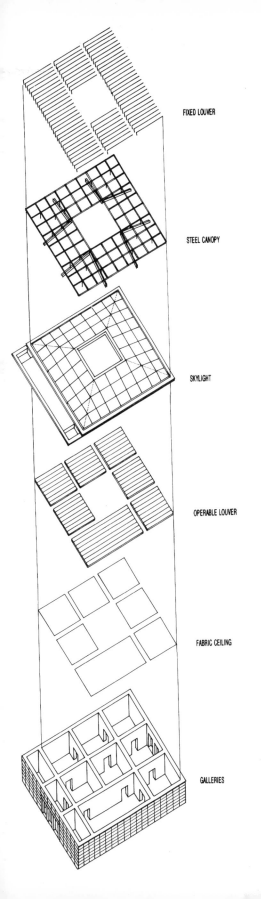

FIXED LOUVER

STEEL CANOPY

SKYLIGHT

OPERABLE LOUVER

FABRIC CEILING

GALLERIES

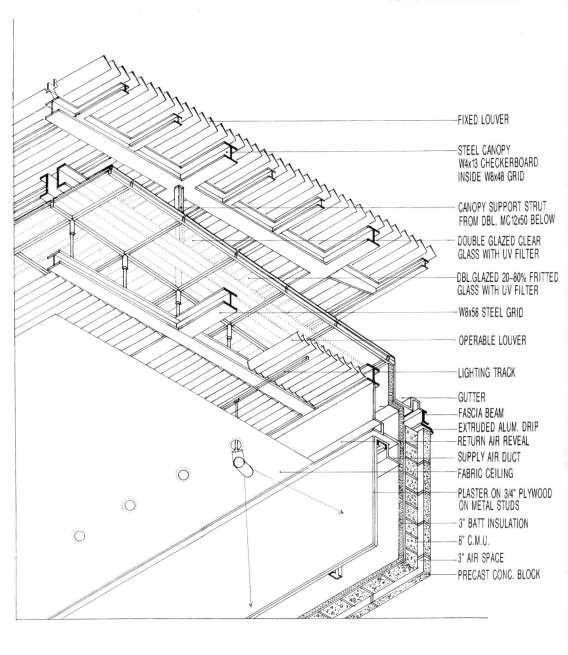

FIXED LOUVER

STEEL CANOPY
W4x13 CHECKERBOARD
INSIDE W8x48 GRID

CANOPY SUPPORT STRUT
FROM DBL. MC12x50 BELOW

DOUBLE GLAZED CLEAR
GLASS WITH UV FILTER

DBL. GLAZED 20–80% FRITTED
GLASS WITH UV FILTER

W8x58 STEEL GRID

OPERABLE LOUVER

LIGHTING TRACK

GUTTER
FASCIA BEAM
EXTRUDED ALUM. DRIP
RETURN AIR REVEAL
SUPPLY AIR DUCT
FABRIC CEILING
PLASTER ON 3/4" PLYWOOD
ON METAL STUDS
3" BATT INSULATION
6" C.M.U.
3" AIR SPACE
PRECAST CONC. BLOCK

Detail of the finishes. Exterior walls are clad in artificial stone.

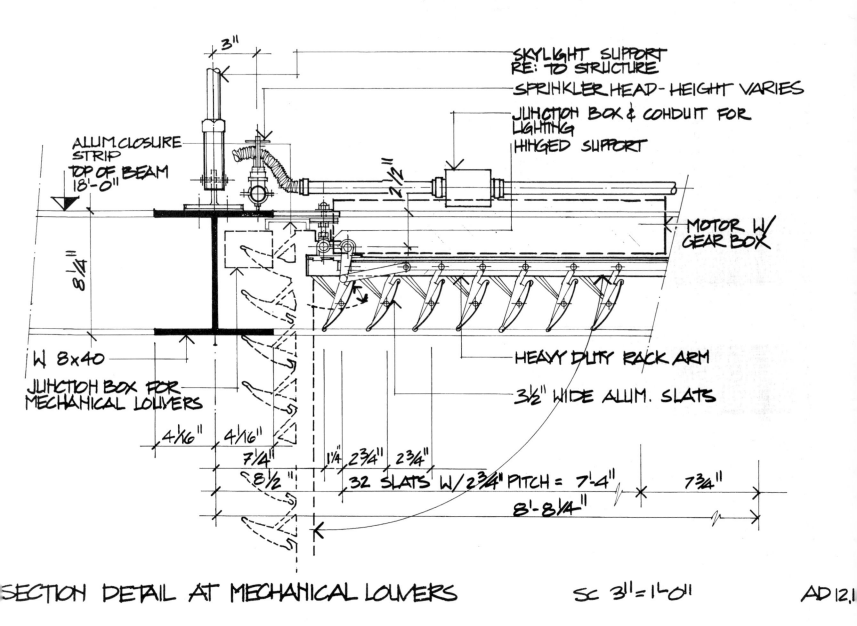

SKYLIGHT SUPPORT
RE: TO STRUCTURE

SPRINKLER HEAD- HEIGHT VARIES

JUNCTION BOX & CONDUIT FOR LIGHTING

HINGED SUPPORT

3"

ALUM. CLOSURE STRIP
TOP OF BEAM
18'-0"

2½"

MOTOR W/ GEAR BOX

8¼"

W 8x40

HEAVY DUTY RACK ARM

3½" WIDE ALUM. SLATS

JUNCTION BOX FOR MECHANICAL LOUVERS

4/16" 4/16"
7¼"
8½"

1¼" 2¾" 2¾"

32 SLATS W/ 2¾" PITCH = 7'-4"   7¾"

8'-8¼"

SECTION DETAIL AT MECHANICAL LOUVERS   SC 3"=1'-0"   AD 12.1

Construction section of the movable slats.

1. Skylight support.
2. Sprinkler head.
3. Joint and light conduit.
4. Hinge.
5. Movable arm.
6. 3 1/2" aluminum strips.